To all my dear friends who have helped make this reality of Divinity and sacred vibration an impressionable labor of love for me for all eternity…I send you blessings across all dimensions. To my beloved husband, daughter and son—you know my deepest love and gratitude for allowing me your gentle presence in this lifetime and for whatever journey is ahead of us…you are my light and inspiration.

To my loving and constant companion, Divine Father and your angels, deepest gratitude for your protection, presence, and unconditional love, which I shall always endeavor, in your Sacred Name, to shine your light for others on earth.

Namaste

Contents

Introduction	vii
Chapter 1 – What I discovered on my way to Wonderland	1
Chapter 2 – New Reality Unveiled with Sacred DNA	19
Chapter 3 – Incarnation (aka) Soul Recycling	33
Chapter 4 – What's the big deal about Lessons	47
Chapter 5 – Motivation for Lessons	53
Chapter 6 – Relationships	69
Chapter 7 – Testimony to God is Alive and Well	85
Chapter 8 – Spirituality vs. Religiousness	107
Chapter 9 – God Indoctrination	117
Chapter 10 – The Blending of Science & Divine Father	123
Chapter 11 – Divine Energy Acceleration – Vibration	131
Chapter 12 – New Age Vibration and Indigo Children	155
Chapter 13 – Gear Up for the Ascension Exercises	171
Appendix A: Instruments for measuring Vibrational energy	*187*
Appendix B: Resources for your Spiritual Journey and Bibliography	*191*
Appendix C: History of Crystal Intelligence	*199*
Appendix D: Scale of Consciousness (Pocket Guide)	*205*
About the Author	*207*

Introduction

DIVINE WONDERLAND: Shedding Light on an Exciting New Reality

✵ ✵ ✵

When Your Vibration shifts, what you perceive in life opens up to a whole new Wonderland of Divine "never before" Experiences.

✵ ✵ ✵

HAVEN'T SOME OF US LOOKED IN THE mirror and said to the reflection staring back at us, "who am I beneath this flesh?"

Now with enlightened research we have answered ***the*** question.

Our Vibration defines us. DNA—both types—our spiritual light-energy body, coupled with our natural-man energy body sets us up for what we are able to perceive. What I have discovered is our true identity is caught between realities of frequency and wavelength—duality of dimensions—there was a time when lower and heavier vibrations were needed in order for us to incarnate our bodies. We live in a 3D world, but much like an action figure in a movie we live dual perceptions of ourselves. We are unlimited beings who have signed up for a human experience.

What happens to us when we are no longer content to rely on the heavier, dense vibration of the human body to dictate how our life unfolds? We start looking for something we can't quite grasp, we look for answers that feel just out of our reach…we think the fantastical is beyond our understanding or we turn to substances to anesthetize ourselves because we are so unhappy with our current perception of things.

Vibration-frequency-wavelength is everything to spirit. That was our natural form. It is STILL always and foremost our natural form. We are Divine energy—and the only thing out of whack with us is our perceptions are being dulled by the human experience we are having.

Most of the time our rational self-talk is tromping on our lives. Ego is having its merry way with us. If you have ever said to someone else or thought to yourself—"I'm stressed out," or "I'm depressed," or "I have no energy,"—then the simple answer is to change your vibration.

You say to yourself—this is almost too simple to believe. Believable or not this is Divine truth.

Think about all the times you have ever said to someone else or thought to yourself—"I'm not as successful as I'd like to be," or "I wish I could find love," or "I wish someone, just anyone understood me and knew what I was going through."

Your instincts are pleading to the heavens for help with your spiritual vibration rate, and by picking up this book to your vibration identity with its path to enlightenment—take heart—it is definitely meant for you to find and discover for yourself the truth.

We now know our Vibration can be measured and altered and can be used to love, heal, protect and transform. So if you have ever wondered about…

* *Where you come from.*
* *Why you are on earth.*
* *What your purpose to this life is.*
* *What your energy vibration means to you.*
* *Why you have been waiting all your life for answers.*

Well, the simple most important thing you can do for yourself is change your energy vibration. All else falls into place after this.

Developing your Divine Vibration is the self-empowering tool to get reacquainted with your true Divine identity. When we realize we are more than human bodies then we can begin to see how we are capable of so much more. I encourage the reader to see his/herself as created by Divine Spirit and that we are all on our own individual paths to finding our purpose here on earth. I reveal the difference between Ego perspective and Spirit perspective. I teach acceptance of our own unique timing with Divine Father (Divine Essence) so that we don't have to be made to feel wrong about our spiritual perspective. This is not a book about religion or judgment. Divine Essence Vibration resides outside the limited perceptions of religion.

The best way to CHANGE OUR LIFE is by raising our frequency or vibration level so that we begin to feel the difference in our energy. When we are operating from a higher vibration we start to view life with a fresh outlook. Our perceptions undergo a startling transformation. The fantastical becomes everyday reality. This positive elevation of awareness is key to spiritual transformation for all mankind.

From my many years of spiritual knowledge and personal transformation, I'm pleased to bring to the reader easy access tools for their path to a happier, content, more rounded life perception.

I provide scientific data and research to my claims that changing your vibration will change your life.

Before I get too far ahead of myself here, let me start from the beginning of my story and tell you a little bit about how I got to where I am now. The events in my story are true events. They have not been altered or changed or otherwise fabricated for any purpose other than the unveiling of our true identity. If my story can assist you in any way in finding your own Divine meaning and identity then I feel blessed to be of service to you.

If you find my story meaningful to your own personal quest, you may wish to further your research into the heart of the matter with what knowledge you have gained here for the last stage.

In my next book, ***Warp Speed to Vibration Wonderland and Beyond,*** I reveal how I knew I was onto something exciting when I sat down to my computer and noticed that my vibration changed the color of my monitor screen. You will be doing your own vibration transformation, too, when you begin to dial into your innate energy frequency.

✳ ✳ ✳

What others have to say about *Divine Wonderland:*

I first met Grace at a class I was teaching on the Sacred Ceremony—Awakening the Divine Essence. Come to find out this kindred soul and I have similar missions in life. I highly recommend her book and how she validates, very well, where we are at in the human evolution to awakening and discovering who we really are, which is DIVINE! Her book comes to you in this season of life about remembering who you are! I am Blessed to have her in my life!

— Lisa Keyes, **www.lisakeyesmdm.com**

Note: This book is an interactive tool designed with extra space after paragraphs where you can hand-write in your personal comments or notes to come back to later to see if your perception might have undergone a change. It is amazing to see ourselves undergo elevated vibration shifts and how our old thoughts might have changed. Have fun with this and enjoy.

✳ ✳ ✳

Chapter 1

What I discovered on my way to Wonderland

I WISH I HAD BEEN ABLE TO find all my life discoveries in one place. Within the pages of one volume of knowledge. That would have been simple. Instead, what I found is knowledge is gathered along the way—by learning through experiences of life. One piece of data leads you on a path of discovery to another piece of knowledge and so on and so forth. This book is a condensed version of my path to enlightenment and knowledge. The reason for my sharing this with you is not for some entertainment factor, but to reconnect you with a lost part of yourself. The time for this information to be revealed to you is now—or you wouldn't have been instinctually drawn to pick up this volume—it is vital for your understanding of your identity and what you are capable of doing and being.

If you have ever heard "when the student is ready, the teacher will materialize" then you recognize you are about to embark on a journey. This book is a culmination of the many teachers moving into my life since around the time I was 23 years old—and what an adventure it has been. I had no idea the extent of what I'd be learning during this latter 32 years of my life or how it would lead to revealing spiritual vibration or spiritual renewal for all of mankind. This book is devoted to you. Because *you* are special enough.

Apart from living life, for many years I've been a student of human behavior, ego, emotions, ambitions and motivations. Haven't we all been students of life? As a student of life I have found out that all the aspects of human ego, human emotions, human ambitions, human motivations, human behaviors, sickness and mental illness is not where the meat of things is.

The more vitally important aspect of who you and I are have more to do with things that can't be nicely labeled, or seen with the naked eye, or inspected under a microscope or even diagnosed by a doctor or any other human for that matter. For the sake of this book and understanding, I'll be speaking to you at a soul vibration level that you might have lost touch with.

To lay some ground work, I need to clarify that in our earthly universe there are a mix of humans either operating mostly out of left brain—analytical thought and concepts or those of us operating out of right brain—abstract thought and intuitiveness.

If you are predisposed to mostly left-brain concepts—everything for you needs to be orderly and in black and white.

On the flip side of this is those predisposed to a built-in intuitiveness that comes with a knowingness about certain things. Most of us don't know why we just know something. A lot of mankind thrive on having everything orderly and in black and white. There is certainly a place and time for orderliness. The problem with this is when people become stuck—or when one can't think outside the safety net of black and white. When someone comes along and upsets these folks orderly, black and white world they make a lot of noise about it. Every one of us have, at some time in our lives, been this person and know someone else or have come across someone else who becomes upset about hearing new concepts. Out of this "orderly, black and white" group come some very rigid and legalistic-minded and stuck ideas of how things work.

Then there are those of us who come along and ask questions of this group and the left-brain or stuck individual goes on the defense; they get his or her nose bent out of shape. For many years I looked at these contrasting people with a tilt of my head and wondered why they just couldn't see outside their safe little box they have built for themselves. Well there is a reason for this, too. It has more to do with our duality, the *ego* side of us. I'll get into that more latter.

For the most part, I have spent years running into other people's boxes.

During this course of time, uniquely, the universe has supplied me with an abundance of teachers. In order to find myself, my identity, I somehow knew I had to keep searching. My brief glimpses of experiences gathered to my breast have been many—in sixth grade I remember being baptized Mormon. I also dabbled in Catholicism with a girlfriend who attended Catholic Church. Even later in high school, I participated in the Methodist youth group in my hometown and was this time baptized Christian. Instincts kept me unsatisfied though, and after just having graduated high school, my boyfriend and I delved into the study of the human mind in Dianetics—in that day and age we learned a lot by hanging out with other like-minded people. But nothing seemed to resonate in a lasting way; something always *felt* a little off kilter.

It wasn't until the dramatic shift in my life during my second marriage that my first and most notable teacher moved into my path—the renowned mystic and healer, Betty Bethards.

At this particular point in life, I started to develop this knowingness that my existence in the world evolved around a bigger picture than the one belonging to limited perceptions.

Today, I'm confident enough about my identity to tell you the God (Divine Father) we hear about from the black and white perspective, introduced to us by religion in general, is more about the Divine Father who lives outside the "boxed-in religions" and He lives outside human-devised boxes. Simply put and as hard as it may be to believe—this means *He* is a God of *all* humankind—not favoring one person over another, not giving special attention to any singular religious group over another, but God loving all of us—regardless our deeds or race or limiting beliefs.

Wow—now isn't that a huge contrast to the general belief out in the community? You're thinking that I better have something really concrete to say to back up my courageous declaration. You could even argue—what about what I have heard in church? What about what I've been hearing over and over from family and friends?

The best way to explain is this—even if we put blinders on, we will at some point in our travels through this life, find our understanding of something will undergo a transformation or shift. Meaning whatever we think we know today can and will change. If this is not happening for you then you're just temporarily stuck. I'm not saying that being stuck is a bad thing, it's just where you are at—understanding something is all about vibrational timing—Divine Father's timing. Between you and Him. If you look closely, you find this takes all the judgment out of it. This is not about anyone judging you—it's about your own personal timing on your path to your identity. All I'm here to do is offer you a fresh perspective so you can begin to see the Divine New Reality that sits there waiting for us to raise our vibration high enough to start seeing with new vision the amazing realm unfold before us. What you do with your discoveries is about your timing and spiritual instincts. If you are not ready it is okay. If you *are* ready then you just are.

Looking at your heritage in Spiritual DNA is where you can start anew—it's about you having a choice.

Choosing something else to consider, is about the nice built-in factor of free will.

Reading from these pages is a personal experience you can have with yourself—with no judgment attached.

No ego gets in the way, unless that's the place from where you've decided you wish to view this new information.

Perhaps you're skeptical and undecided. I say that's okay. So now for the moment try this—read on and see if you don't start to feel yourself expanding and growing beyond the limiting beliefs.

It all starts with our thoughts on things. What we think or perceive about something. This is going to sound a little strange, but more important than what's going on around you right now or what you've seen on the news today—is you.

You develop you—you get to start understanding who you are—and if you *want* or *desire* to be "unstuck" then you will start to see things you never saw or perceived before.

Your perceptions widen to take in so much more.

Doors that you haven't been able to move beyond will be opened, things you desire flow into you effortlessly, answers to questions will be forthcoming. The simple universal law of "free will" will start to become clearer to you—you'll start to understand why Divine Father set the universe up like this for us.

Your spiritual growth and mine depend upon our gentle and successful transformation into this new unit of Divine time. The day is upon all mankind where the shift in spiritual consciousness is awakening within each of us; the time in our history where we as spiritually evolving humans start to see and hear more about the evolving nature of science and our spiritual identity coming to a head.

This special time of spiritual transformation requires all mankind to grasp the larger concept of blending into the essence of what Divine Father needs for all of us to do right here, starting right now. If you are wanting and desiring answers, then there's no more time for those old, ego-arrogant belief systems we pack around with us.

Universal spirit consciousness is the single most vital concept demanded of us right now today—no longer should we be allowing ourselves to skate through life being prejudice of one person over another or one religion over another. Holding onto those old ego-based concepts isn't going to better our planet conditions—only the new concept of joined consciousness of Divine Father will get us through upcoming storms.

And if you need reminding that there are storms brewing then go back to listening to the news.

Go back to listening to what's happening in the world, the economy, the neighbor who hasn't worked for months, the recent death toll from a massive flood, the hungry and starving families—and you feel the weight of the suffering.

Believe it or not we each can do something about what we see. We can have a voice and we can be *felt* by those needing us.

If you're in a place where you have all you can do to keep your head above water, then you can relax, because we understand you aren't yet in a place where you are expected to do anything but carry on with your own growth.

Oh, and by the way, you do have a divine purpose you are here fulfilling for yourself. For now, I am going to introduce you to the essence of *who you really are*. The extent of *who you really are*. Give you some fresh concepts and tools on the path to finding your true identity.

It all started for me the day I desired and wanted to help others who, just like me, weren't satisfied with the same old answers. It was a time not that long ago when I was conceiving I would have to write a book on Spiritual DNA identity. It started with me having a dickens of a time trying to settle on a title for this book while a spiritual friend kept after me to hurry up and write it. I wrote some—let it "ferment", and then I wrote a little more. The reason this story has taken its *God timing* was I had to undergo a new stage of enlightenment pretty much as each chapter was being formed. I now know why. It's a larger story than any I had started out with. Because it's about mankind's lost heritage, it started to morph into something larger than life and death itself.

The reason it's larger than any of the limiting circumstances we are faced with—it's not about the things going on around us at any given time—it's about what's on the inside. It's about our true inner identity. This is where your answers to everything in this life reside. The search isn't "out there" it's "in here" inside. It's about finding *you*. The "*you*" inside your body suit.

There are a lot of books and teachers out there who have their identity figured out and have written books about it.

Heck, the whole array of modern day Bibles (circa 1300-1350)—all nine hundred interpretations are about our identity—that's if you are able to read between the lines and you have an interpreter who has their identity figured out. It's worth reiterating here so let me say again, it's not anyone's place to judge the teacher, it's more about where your teacher is at spiritually.

What you listen to happens to be where you're presently at spiritually. It's just a present level of awareness. The nice thing about this is your awareness is capable of expanding and transforming hourly, daily, and monthly using your free will. Here's the thing—the big secret is out there. There is no right or wrong way to how you get you identity figured out. I repeat—NO right or wrong way. It becomes your particular way of doing it. Custom fit to you. It just becomes about different stages of understanding and enlightenment going on. To make one person right or wrong is *us* dwelling in human ego. Being spiritual is to see the stages of development for what they are. Just temporary stages. We are all in one stage or another all the time. Some of us can be in overlapping stages simultaneously. It becomes about the "gray" area. Divine Father resides in the gray area. He *is* the gray area. It's the unexplained area. Undefined area. No mere black and white words fashioned by human capacity can explain gray area. Meaning He can't be confined to black and white definition. We try our very best to capture Him, as well as our own spirit essence within black and white definition, but alas we merely skim the surface of understanding. But, this is where you must take heart. With Divine identity intact everything becomes possible. I've paraphrased this—God left no one out when He said, *"With me everything is possible."*

Everything means everything. I am my own testimony as I will reveal to you. You are included in "everything"—your spiritual heritage is intact whether you see it with your ego or not. So back to what took me so long to write this book for you. Well, part of it had to do with my own personal spiritual unfoldment which goes without saying, it has taken me some time to figure out how I wanted to use myself as an example. You may have heard how Jesus used all sorts of characters of all reputations and varied backgrounds to tell His stories. There are a lot of modern day Divine stories that are bible-worthy. I have often said, I would love to have heard Lazarus' story from his point of view. But alas, with current day publishing technologies and a platform called the internet, we can tell our stories in this new unit of God time.

Back to how come it took me so long to get this book out—the other part that took so long in the making has been what I've researched on all our behalves.

Divine Father seems to be nudging me to be supplied with truths.

When I recognized this, which comes with a daunting responsibility when relaying things of a divine nature, I realized there had to be other people just like me who might want some ideas on how to go about obtaining answers. Which, for each of us is how we are conceived. It's directly tied to *who you are inside* the body suit you pack around with you all day.

If you've ever had the pleasure of watching the movie *"Mother Teresa"* staring Oliva Hussey, you saw how Divine intervention unfolded in her life. Not until after watching that movie and seeing it played out before me on a screen did I realize I had parallels occurring in my life. When I finally saw some sort of parallels going on, and me an ordinary person, I was thrilled that I had followed an inclination to watch the movie. Because the more I became conscious of this intangible Divine flow and I became secure in Divine intervention, the more it seemed to love to show itself off to me. Divine intervention becomes the noun in this case. For the times I just waited like an expectant child for a glimpse of the Divine fairy dust to fall on me, I was never let down. The more I used this and cultivated habits of reliance on this wonderfully developing Divine connection the more it showed up in my day. It's always been there. If only I had learned reliance on my Divine connection sooner. This is why I write this book. To share the way to tap into this Divine connection we all have access to. I'm hoping with some of the tools I've used, you can easily cultivate the divine access you're entitled to. First things first though, is your willingness to suspend disbelief.

Whether or not you are one-hundred percent invested in the concept of your own Divine connection, you can count on this: Always, Divine Father is right here with us.

Maybe, like me, you just need to exercise your spiritual muscles to get your connection going. It's like having a computer and not knowing how to use the thing. There are frustrating moments for sure.

But when it works, boy is it exhilarating. For me, I made it kind of like a game, the more I used my Divine access muscle the more toned it got, until strangely, I finally one day figured out if I learned to rely on Divine intervention muscles, I wasn't going to be disappointed. Now for the tricky part. You must have the eyes to see and the ears to hear. I have learned over and over that our Divine Father is a very doting father, and the more I relied upon Him (seeing just what He might bring to me), the more He seemed to enjoy it.

Divine Father has given me the most unexpected and wonderfully creative wishes answered. I'm reminded of when Betty Bethards told of her amusing story with her grass field needing plowed and all she had in her hand was a rake. Her story will stay with me forever—how Divine Spirit answered her with a really humorous turn of events that led to her field getting plowed by a farmer who accidentally drove his tractor onto her property while he was tilling his own. All this happened unbeknownst to her since she had gone off to the hardware store. When she got back she couldn't believe her eyes. God had answered her silent prayer. She told countless stories just like this. I have seen this! For myself. Don't be fooled into thinking this is a thing called coincidence. I'll talk about the difference between coincidence and divine intervention later. The more spiritual you become, the more you understand that there are *no* coincidences. So now—aren't you just a little bit curious about tapping into some of this for yourself?

When you are given a miracle or something in the shape of divine intervention, please do not forget to thank Divine Father. Even if you think it's just a coincidence, go ahead and thank Divine Father.

Trust me, He's listening and waiting to see if we get it. He's waiting for us to figure out that there *are no coincidences.* I've spent a great deal of time training that muscle too, to always be paying attention to how the answer to something will be granted.

If I look even closer, which I've also trained myself to do, then I see just how the answer incorporated the big picture. Sometimes the answer is so unexpected in its ingenuity that I don't immediately see how it was the best answer. Haven't you heard someone say, "Well, I prayed for it, but my prayer went unheard or He doesn't hear me or He doesn't seem to care." If you have ever said this about your own prayer, my guess is that you completely missed the divine reply/answer. How do we miss the answer? Because we want to place our own control of the outcome into the equation. Face it, ego wants things its way. Aren't we usually like that? Wanting things our own way? Well, when we miss Divine Fathers answer, that's exactly what we get. It's the law of free will. We get a human-tampered-with answer to the prayer. The other possibility is we just can't see how Divine

Father would answer us the way He did, so we *ignore* the miracle loaded with possibility coming our way. It's like we don't see the forest at all for all the human-erected trees. Read on and I just might be able to help you get yourself out of the way of finding the miracles happening in your own life.

How this prayer process works for myself is, I spend a requisite moment or two ruminating on what it is I need—call it a mental prayer. Then I simply relax all my own expectations and inclinations about how I want it to turn out (this is key) and I simply allow it to materialize in whatever fashion Divine Father sees best. So even when I'm just wishing for something, I find it materializing. Always, the answer materializes, in inventive new ways.

This is pretty cool when I realized at some point along the road, I was really calling upon and calling forth that stuff they talk about in law of attraction references. Here's the deal—only if you are able to overcome your own limiting perceptions or sometimes it is someone else's limiting perceptions interjected upon you, will you be able see the correlation between law of attraction and God's divine presence at work. It's just another one of those pieces to God's puzzle.

This manifestation of ideas, wishes or prayers, whatever name you wish to attach to them, they also come with a huge responsibility in using thoughts wisely. There are some great new references out there that go into the explanation of how vital our thoughts are, how the emotional energy you give the thought is as vital as the thought itself to how we are making our lives unfold.

What we tell ourselves with our feelings attached is a bigger problem than we ever would have guessed—so we need to learn to edit thought to change our circumstances. Emotional energy is a subject that deserves its very own book, and there has been much laboratory research to validate the power of thought. Thoughts in a nutshell can hold us back or free us. In this material I'm presenting here, you will be learning how to change your life and limiting perceptions of yourself by use of thought. That is to say, you'll be learning how, if you wish, to modify and edit your vibrational perceptions of things (thoughts).

Like Betty Bethards did, I'll give you a brief example. One day on my way to my other job, I was talking on the phone with my friend, and I had a thought or epiphany about how I needed more data for this book. I posted, with feeling, my thought out there.

It wasn't a week later when at work, another one of those teachers in my life materialized, thank you Herman, and he spoke of Sacred Geometry. Now you have to understand I studied a little geometry in college, and I found it incredibly boring in the context of algebra. But now here in real life I found it suddenly intriguing and wanted to know more. Divine timing is what I call it.

Chapter 2

New Reality Unveiled with Sacred DNA

HERE'S WHERE I GET INTO THE HEART of who you and I are. I can pretty much bet, you intuitively picked up this book not yet knowing or realizing why, but you did so either instinctively or for some unknown reason. That reason, maybe undetected by your conscious mind, is sometimes called a "knowingness". At the very least it is an inherited "eagerness" to discover the truth to who you are. These hunches sometimes come with no rhyme or reason, just pure intuition. Not to fret—what you are searching for will very likely be revealed here. It may be unexpected. At the very least some of it may sound familiar while other parts just seem to resonate with you on a deeper level. If you can suspend disbelief and are willing to entertain fresh ideas then perhaps this book is just the beginning unturned stone on your path.

Remember, you do not need to or have to believe everything you read or hear or see. Your timing with spirit self is not dependent on this book. As any spiritually-connected soul will advise you: take with you what resonates with you and discard what doesn't. Your timing is between you and Divine Father.

I've decided to write this, not necessarily for the person who feels more comfortable with their own spiritual resources, but for those, who like myself, needed better answers. Maybe you're the person who had a very unpleasant "religion" experience or you have been turned off by the traditional means of receiving spiritual insight.

I guarantee you, I'm just an ordinary person. I've got an ordinary job, a day job aside from writing. Everything about me is ordinary. Maybe the only thing that is different about you and I, is my inexplicable realization about my spiritual heritage, and that I've invested time in developing myself spiritually. I know you are maybe expecting someone great and worldly. But I claim no fame for myself. I'm just a simple messenger.

The glory belongs to Divine Spirit alone. I am created "in His image" (Genesis 1:27), just as you are.

That makes us children of Divine Spirit, or Father God, or whatever name you personally have attached to your spiritual creator.

I know this much: we are ordinary divine spirits having a human experience. Human experience means we have taken on or incarnated into a human body.

And just like millions of other divine spirit persons who inhabit this earth in our earth suits, who are looking for answers, now seems to be the time you have decided you are ready for a new journey.

Sometimes spiritual journeys can reveal things that make us uncomfortable. Spiritual journeys can also reveal much if a person is ready and willing to listen. Betty Bethards was famous for saying we just have to have the eyes to see and the ears to hear for enlightenment to dawn on us. Some readers of this book, will of course, be happy to read this material for the entertainment factor and then do nothing else with the knowledge. That is our free will exercising itself, it's our own individual choice.

We'd all like clear definitions, scientific answers to all that is going on in our lives. But the plain truth is some things just can't be explained. For instance, researchers still can't explain or see precisely what's happening at an atomic energy level inside the Golgi Body of a human cell. This doesn't mean there's nothing going on inside the Golgi Body. It just means we can't see it with the human eye or with our most powerful microscopes, yet.

Another example—it wasn't until just recently, sometime mid-year 2013, that the special Animal Planet documentary on mermaids shocked a lot of us with the scientific data and live footage captured on film. It pretty much revealed to us that, *"with God all things are possible."* (Matthew 19:26) Again, I use this as an example to bring home the point that just because we haven't seen things under our very noses, doesn't mean they don't exist. Of course, there's the ego-driven person, operating out of fear, who will refute even things they see in plain sight.

Hey, I say we are entitled to our own rate of spiritual development, this is our God-given free will choice. So where are you at? Belief or disbelief. This is a measuring stick to how much work you have left to do on yourself—that's all it is.

You can probably think of a whole bunch of instances where you wondered about something you couldn't see—I think we all have. It didn't stop us from intuitively thinking "there's more to it than meets the eye." So just because we can't *see* Spiritual DNA with the naked eye, it doesn't mean it's not there inside each of us. There is current day scientific means of measuring some of this phenomenon.

One author, Lynne McTaggart, has done a wonderful job of compiling for us this specialized area of research called Quantum Physics in terms that readers can follow.

If you care to venture there, her book is full of what I view as Divine phenomenon and scientific testimonies of who we are as spiritual beings. We'll get into some of the other scientifically measured and proven spiritual phenomena as we go along in the next chapters. Sacred Geometry, Spiritual vibration/resonance, Light-body energy phenomenon and Spontaneous Healing are but a few of the exciting areas into which we will venture. Yes, and we will go into the specialized area of the spiritual mind of Indigo Children. We will get a look at what heaven looks like from some of those who have traveled there and back with information to share with us all. Again, it's too bad we didn't get to hear in the Bible what Lazarus might have had to tell us about his personal experience. You see I'm leaving very little out; we are embarking on this spiritual adventure together to enable you to develop your spiritual muscles.

Let's talk now about DNA for a moment. A logical place to start with is the biological kind we get from our natural parents, also known as our biological parents. So what is this DNA stuff? Why is it important to mankind?

First let's say, if you were to have gene markers identified within your DNA they would tell you a little bit about what your biological parents have passed on to you.

DNA tells us a good deal about what eye color, skin color, and shape we will get from our parents as well as some of the less desired characteristics and this is just the tip of the iceberg about what we know. As much as science has discovered what it is that makes up genetic DNA, there are just as many unanswered questions remaining. Five years ago, I was told by my college instructor that there is only half of our DNA identified. That means there was still a mystery surrounding the other half.

This means there is still much to learn, and though we haven't yet been told the answers, I tend to believe the unidentified DNA is still there for a reason. That this mysterious DNA isn't just taking up space or given to us by some freak-of-nature accident. Again, just because I can't explain the DNA that hasn't been identified doesn't mean DNA isn't busy performing some vital function.

Now that we have taken a walk down the path to exercise the fact that we can't see things going on right under our very noses, I'm taking things a step further and bringing *spirit* into the mix.

Simply put, Spiritual DNA is about genes given to us by our *spiritual parent*—our spiritual creator.

If talking about our *spiritual parent* makes you a little uncomfortable then my bet is you're not alone—you're probably among a good portion of the population. So, I beg your indulgence here.

Okay, let's for the moment entertain the notion that we are trying to overcome our programmed beliefs and disillusions and fears about the name and existence of our spiritual parent. I've already mentioned His name a few times to get you accustomed to this exciting venture. By now all of you know whom I'm talking about—I'm talking about how you've probably decided on who your maker is and what His name is, what religion He belongs to and what common belief says He looks like.

Just so you know where I stand—you remember earlier I talked about how I have personally tried on a few religions.

Since those days, I have adopted a consciousness that I am of Divine spiritual essence, which belongs to no secular religion but instead to Divine Presence—also referred to as Divine Father. I could reference Divine Father interchangeably to suit all religions across the board and I would be putting the same heartfelt emphasis to the meaning—Divine Father of all mankind, regardless of deed or race. When I reference one religion it is merely my familiarity with that religion; it is for emphasis of a particular point I'm wanting to get across without having to reference or list by name all the different spiritual religions or texts.

Now that we have the fundamental pieces of the picture laid out, let's move on.

By definition, DNA –Deoxyribonucleic Acid— (molecules strung together in a double helix strand) is the hereditary stuff we get from our human parents. When one defines *spiritual DNA*—well now I've ventured into the area of the "unseen by the naked eye or human eye." Capturing Divine energy or presence with scientific validity, has been an ongoing project of many a Scientist since the beginning of creation.

Very timely and so that I don't have to incorporate here all the research needed to prove the Divine Energy who *is you and I*, I have acquainted myself with the many pioneers who have laid down some ground work for us. One such person is Gregg Braden, best-selling author of *The God Code* and leading authority on bridging the wisdom of our past with science, medicine, and peace of our future.

He has researched the hidden meaning of Divine Father's name as it is encoded into our human bodies.

Gregg Braden's research has uncovered the DNA (hydrogen, nitrogen, oxygen, and carbon molecules) that directly translate into specific letters of the Hebrew alphabet—YHVA—which in turn translates into one of the original names of God. Jonathan Goldman, an internationally known writer and authority on sound healing, in collaboration with Gregg Braden's research, has developed the sound of the *God Code*.

According to Jonathan and Gregg, the Kabbalah, the personal name of God is sacred and more than 2,300 years ago, God's sacred name was removed from the religious texts that link over one half of the world's population in order to safeguard its use. We have much to be thankful to them for.

Since, according to Jonathan, it is through their collaboration efforts that the personal name of God, encoded within the DNA of all life, has been reproduced with the human voice in its original form so that now you and I can experience the power, mystery, and healing of The Divine Name, re-created through the sounds that unite, rather than the letters that divide. I thought it pertinent to dust off the CD I own with the sounds of *The God Code* and start listening to it as I wrote this section on DNA. The resonance is palpable—my computer, for no reason at all, shifted from this paragraph in Word Document to the My Documents screen and the smoke alarm we have hanging from our ceilings, well, it started to chirp for no reason at all. I feel God resonating through me. I guess the electronics in my writing room could feel Him, too. Cool, huh!

I'll direct you to another pioneer author, Lynne McTaggart, who explains very neatly this "energy" whom Divine Father instilled in us in her latest book, *The Intention Experiment.* The numerous experiments exemplified in her book use scientific equipment to take measure of spirit energy. Scientific experiments are conducted with control groups and test groups, so that they can prove their findings. One particular experiment that impressed me was what I call the equivalent of a modern day Moses story. Again, using the same energy as bequeathed us by the Divine Presence or God, one test subject demonstrated that physical matter *can* be moved with the Divine mind each of us is born with. This energy is Spiritual DNA at its best.

Simply speaking—it stands to reason we possess two complete sets of DNA. One set from our Spiritual parent and one set from our Human parents.

Again, when I say *spirit,* I am talking about *you-the-spirit* inhabiting the body you are packing around with you on earth.

This is to say, I recognize you aren't the body you dwell in—you are spirit. We have discussed that true to human nature, some people are going to have trouble with this. This happens naturally, since a good number of people probably still think they *are* the body.

However, the more you develop your spiritual identity, the more you are going to see the two are distinctly different. And, remember, if you aren't already aware of this, not a problem. Some day you will be made aware when you leave the body behind you as you take off for the next dimension called spirit world.

With that distinction made and out of the way we can begin.

Why is Spiritual DNA important? Who cares one way or another, anyway? Why does any of this matter, you ask?

Again to give emphasis to the importance—this book is about you and me and everyone who wants to understand why we are here on earth. So we can begin to understand why things seem to "happen" to us. Understand why we complain about the unfairness of life. These, again, are just our limited perceptions of what is taking place. The truth about things is just a different perception. The "aha" moment is a skill, with the right tools, which anyone can develop. This book is not just for some of us, it's for all of us. This book is about awakening you to that which is the governing law of all life—Spirit governs all.

This is the brand new dawn of enlightenment. If you haven't been drawn to any particular religion or following one up to now, you may be one of those persons who only have so much time to get tapped into some Divine connection and get in touch with who you are before you leave the body behind (clinically called death). You can start at any point of your life. Young or old. Most people wait to ask spirit questions only when their human body is diseased, sick, or beginning to die.

Whoever you are, you should be paying close attention to persons who talk of universal love and acceptance. You can overcome your present mode of operation by moving from your present ego-based consciousness into your more divine spiritual consciousness. We are a living, breathing duality of consciousness. Ego vs. Spirit. That's us in a nutshell.

If you are feeling alone, afraid, trapped, going insane, then shift yourself. From ego- to spirit-consciousness.

Understanding why we are a living, breathing conflict of two parts of self, is the beginning to understanding what we are up against when human-based consciousness overrides the spirit self. Ego underlies everything we do. To operate on earth, we took on the ego and body. It has not made us any happier. In fact, we are not necessarily here to be happier. We each have our own reasons and purposes to be incarnated. And here you've probably thought you were just a random happenstance. You will learn different if you so choose. For the first time in earth history, mankind is starting to awaken from its amnesia. We are more attuned and becoming enlightened. We are recognizing what we have been doing and trying out on ourselves as segregated groups is not working for our benefit or that of the planet.

How do you really change things—STOP DOING THE *SAME* THINGS. Doing the same behaviors, habits, holding firmly to the same old ego-serving beliefs and EXPECTING DIFFERENT RESULTS, is foolish and will keep us following down the present path of going nowhere. The good news is this fatalistic behavior is unnecessary. You and I have been created with the same Divine minds we inherited from our Divine Father.

Only by educating ourselves and evolving our spirit self, and thus, pulling together collectively are we going to get into balance with the natural man state or ego state, and move beyond believing we are just flesh and blood bodies walking around on earth. Why is this important? Of course survival means different things to each of us. For those of you who think you are just bodies, you may be caught up in earth time survival—this present life we are living—while in your body. Spiritual survival IS the bigger picture. Among many who are awakening to their purposes, my personal story is testimony for all who wish to awaken themselves from the amnesia, which is part of the human experience, and I'm happy to reveal my story to you. Since the beginning of time, the stories have been forthcoming. My story is merely a modern day version.

The example that may be most familiar to a great number of people is stories of Jesus' message to us—He has shown us examples of how we should be pulling together to overcome our old patterns of thinking and behaviors towards one another. What I recognized for myself is, every day that passes I have an opportunity to grow myself spiritually.

This is my question to you—are you feeling at a loss? About anything? Are you feeling at times like you are on top of the world and then something comes along to change your day starting that very next morning? You wonder why life has to be a roller-coaster of ups and downs. Have you ever been told that personal peace is attainable? Personal joy is attainable? That it can be a sustained presence in your life? Or are you one of those persons who likes maintaining a life of miserable-ness because it better serves you and your purpose for being here? Remember—I'm not judging here.

Have you given up believing that we can all implement this radical self-transformation vitally required of each of us to heal ourselves before we leave our bodies?

Truth is—the biggest part of our present day mission is going to be accomplished while we are still in our bodies.

Chapter 3

Incarnation (aka) Soul Recycling

THERE ARE MANY UPON MANY STORIES SURFACING of spiritual recognition and identity.

They come in many different forms. Many such stories are related by near death participants like Dannion Brinkley, Anita Moorjani, Dr. Mary Neal, Don Piper, Colton Burpo, Betty Eadie, Betty Bethards, and George Ritchie. Their stories are a mere few of the total big picture talking about the path to self-discovery from the tone of either regrets or enlightenment. These lucky souls (spirits) got a second chance. Maybe you will, too. This is something you may or may not know yet.

Miraculously, as NDE (Near Death Experience) participants, these folks got a second chance to come back into their present earth body and work things out. A Near Death Experience is just another example of incarnating (back into your present body). An example you may have heard about is Lazarus in the Christian Holy Bible scripture. Lazarus did this same kind of spirit incarnating into body experience. His story is some 2,000 years old. And guess what—Divine Father was intimately involved in that incarnation, just as Divine Father is intimately involved in our own incarnations. I think it's too bad we never got to hear Lazarus' personal story in the Bible—what he might have revealed to us from his perspective and whether he might have had, like Dannion Brinkley and the rest, a wealth of wisdom to impart to us. If you can get past your ego objecting to this possibility, then you're ahead of the game.

The most important factor in the above—is what their experiences taught them about themselves as spiritual beings. If you are coming from a place of ego, then I guess you could focus on a number of unimportant facts, like making the person wrong for having their experience. If you are coming from a place of spirit, then you will be able to understand and focus on the more important element and a bigger picture. As a person who knows my own identity, I realize they didn't decide to have the experiences so that they could sell books.

Quite the contrary, the experience happened *to* them. It picked them, so they wrote about their stories to give the rest of us a glimpse at what to look forward to. My story is merely a different aspect on the subject of spirit.

My story has a thread of commonality to us all. Self-talk. The kind of self-talk that hurts us for lifetimes to come until we get it. I had to get that I *was* indeed created in His image. That I am worthy of love. Worthy of respect. I had to learn to love myself enough, to not put myself in harmful relationships. My lesson for me was self-love. My lesson had to do with feeling like I'm enough and that I mattered. The realization I had to get was that I had to respect myself even if the other person wasn't on-board with that.

The common realization for a lot of us is that we don't think we are worthy. This is because we listen to others tell us all the bad things they think about us until we start believing what they say as truth. It has nothing to do with the blanket contract that Divine Father says we are created in His image and therefore worthy of the greatest possible love. Someone else can't just say we are loved and worthy for us to believe it and make it stick. No, it has to be self-realized for it to stick. I don't know about anyone else, but I was pretty stubborn about getting to learn my lesson the hard way. I understand now why I incarnated and the purpose for others to treat me bad enough that I would learn from the best (or worst) that loving myself as Divine Spirit loves me meant that I had to learn the hardest way to love myself enough to not involve myself in demeaning or destructive relationships.

The dynamic involved here is a spiritual pact made with someone on the other side (in spirit realm) who loved me enough to help me evolve myself. Believe it or not, this pact for the enforcer comes at a great cost—being a huge emotional and spiritual sacrifice to them. It pretty much breaks the heart of the Spirit who has to inflict that much grief on a fellow Spirit in order for the other person to get his lesson learned.

Because my ego was getting in the way a lot and making me stubborn, my pain and suffering was imperative for me to spiritually grow to realize the significance of what I had been telling myself one life time after another. In my past lives I had told myself I wasn't worthy of the relationship I was in. I was, basically, not loving myself at those moments.

We must learn to love ourselves as Divine Father loves us. And I'm not talking about the hell, fire, and brimstone God that we have created in our minds at church. I'm talking about our Divine Father whose love is unconditional and unfathomable by any definition made by human standards or written about with human hands.

We defile Him the moment we try to define Him and His love of us. If you have a hard time imaging that unimaginable kind of love pouring forth to us, try this exercise. Look into the eyes of Jesus in the few movies available to us when He is looking at someone with His heart in His eyes and let yourself feel His love pouring onto you in that look. If at first you can't accomplish this exercise just be patient and try it again at another point in the future. It will become easier the more you practice this on other spirits (people) around you. At some point, with enough practice, you will begin to see Jesus in other people's eyes. It's a mutual divine connection. Meaning, you will be felt by others. When you have become one with Divine Father, these people will tell you that there is something about you—they will try to define it. It's your divine kindness and love shining through your eyes to touch them.

For a lot of spiritual souls reading this message, they will get the precise significance to what I'm imparting here and they recognize the gift the other person gave me with their seemingly harsh presence in my life. When we realize we are responsible for our own choices that get us into the trouble we have predestined for ourselves by the pact made on the other side, then we can begin to see more clearly with eyes opened and hearts bare.

When we take all the blame away from the other person and realize we are responsible for the lesson we set up to learn here on earth and that they just simply agreed to help us with great spiritual pain to themselves then we see the other person as very necessary to our growth and that they are giving us the greatest gift possible. The gift we came here for—the one of self-actualized love and respect of ourselves. This is why if you seem to attract the same types of people into your life again and again, it's because your Divine purpose is designed to help you find your way back to the beautiful essence you are even if here on earth you seem to be doing everything in your power to stay on the same path of destruction. You can break the patterns the moment you love yourself as you are designed to love yourself. It's that simple. Believe me, if I can do it, anyone can do it. In the chapter on relationships, I will go into depth about this agreement we make with one another on the other side. I can help maybe clarify a lot of things about why/when we move on from a relationship and when that might or might not be necessary.

Getting back to this business of taking on a human body—or I like to think of it as recycling myself into earth bodies with the help and blessing of Divine Father.

I understand that you might have a hard time believing this is possible. As spirits having a human experience, you-the-ego wants to over-rule any concepts except the black and white ones. So it is understandable that skeptics of this concept are many. However, the good news is, the more you become awakened to your true identity as Spirit the less trouble you will have trusting Divine Spirit world. So it goes without saying that some people will still vehemently oppose this concept. Problem is for these folks, it still doesn't make the fact go away. They just choose to ignore it is all. Again this is your free will choice. If you choose to believe otherwise then that is where you will be. It just is. You are simply in your particular state of spiritual awareness. Neither right nor wrong enters into the place where you are. Your state is just that—it's a state of awareness.

In light of this particular spiritual state of awareness—you could further say you are right about what you know and are aware of. Your statement would be correct. Likewise, I'm just in my own particular state of awareness. That we differ in the states of awareness we are in makes it okay. Just as you do, I have the same right to what I believe at my state of awareness. No one, not myself included should ever say you are wrong about where you are at. We are all here for learning and earth is our playground. We are ever learning and evolving.

So guess what comes next? Judgment, as a whole, then relaxes and allows us to just be the spiritual being that we are. In the state of awareness we are in at the time. Remember though that a person's spiritual state of awareness is subject to possible change at any time. For example, if you should die (meaning your earth suit dies), your spiritual awareness will instantly shift. I think you can safely agree then, that you are merely in a different form at that precise moment you leave your body. Some of us think when our body dies then that's the end to us. If that's your present perception of how things are, that's okay. It doesn't make it truth, however. Just a perception.

For the sake of argument, if you insist on bringing ego into it, then you could say we are both right about what we know for our own truth at the point we are at. This is an unspoken law of spirit world. One based on NO judgment—just unconditional love.

Let me say right here, again, that not everyone needs to follow my recipe for spiritual growth, I'm just giving you my example to look at for one possibility.

Again, some of you will feel uncomfortable with this subject of incarnation and want to put the book down right here. Again, this is your free will choice. Understand that I'm not needing to twist anyone's arm at all. Divine Spirit has as many options for you to follow for growth as there are spiritual concepts available to you.

Of course, once you get over being disillusioned about past lives, you will find there are many authorities on this topic and places to go to for help to relive your own past life experience.

DIVINE WONDERLAND: SHEDDING LIGHT ON AN EXCITING NEW REALITY 41

One such person who can educate you about this subject is Brian L. Weiss, M.D. Dr. Weiss can open unexpected doors into the realm of past-life regression; help you release old phobias and fears from prior lifetimes. If you are ready for this step, there are also other resources for past life clean-up, as well. You just might like to research to find one near you. Now why would looking at a past life make any difference, you ask? From my own personal experience, I can assure you, the significance is more far-reaching than even I expected.

The significance of validating past lives for myself was in the freedom from old programs I carried with me from life to life. *This is why claiming our spiritual identity is so vital to us as spiritual beings.* I will go into this more in depth later and why becoming responsible as divine spiritual beings releases us from being victims in this life.

Betty Bethards, whom I've mentioned earlier, has her own wonderful story of her ND experience and how it lead to her spiritual enlightenment. For the Christian community, in his recent book, *90 Minutes in Heaven*, Pastor Don Piper tells an inspiring story of going out of his body and then coming back into his body (his is another Near Death Experience), and how it led to further spiritual enlightenment for him. Another authority on the matter of past lives is renowned healer, spiritual leader and Medical Doctor, Master Sha. In his book, *Soul Wisdom*, he talks about how the soul enlightenment journey has taken hundreds, even thousands of lifetimes for most souls. He explains how at this time, only 15 percent of humanity are enlightened souls. He also goes on to say that humanity is in a special place in time, Mother earth is undergoing a difficult transition—one he elaborates on for you—and the Divine God needs more enlightened beings to serve humanity.

Let me interject here, I don't presume to call myself one of his "enlightened beings."

Instead let me say again, that if you have been a victim of spiritual identity theft, then all I am doing for us is accepting responsibility that this is where I need to step up to the plate for spiritual identity—for all those of you who are feeling like you are wandering around in the dark about why we are here on this earth and what sense can we make of it. I'm drawing from what I've learned from my past life experiences, as well as the 35-plus years of present life experiences. The timing could be pretty critical to you from a spiritual view—my timing to bring you my voice seems to be now.

I will say right now, as well—instead of being down on yourself, be thankful for the chance to incarnate. Incarnating can mean you get another chance to clear up the horrid things you have perhaps done to others and done to yourself and you get to unload the huge burden of guilt you pack around with you. Although, what I understand of being on the other side, in the spirit dimension, you experience such love as no love on earth and there is no condemnation or judgment by Divine Father, so whether you have an opportunity to reflect on your mistakes made in the human body is probably a mute point.

If all you feel "over there" is unconditional love, then you'll probably give yourself grace any way. The irony is, the only place I have heard of where a person gets to practice on one another how to clear things up is down here on earth. This is where we get to clean up our mistakes by practicing them upon others. This is where our *free will* choices can either get us in a lot more trouble or be our free ticket home. This is where treating each other with love, compassion, and respect comes into play. Also, be forewarned right now, because what I've learned and understand of it, if you think suicide is your free ticket home, you are going to be sorely disappointed.

Killing off your earth suit does not help you skip the lessons you've incarnated to clear up. Sadly, the opposite happens.

Sadly, you get to come back and relive the circumstances that led right up to your self-inflicted death. I can understand, though, how some life experiences can make you feel such hopelessness and trapped in circumstances that you feel you can no longer bear it. I've been in that place. I, luckily, kept telling myself that something had to get better. Maybe part of it had to do with my knowledge of what suicide meant in terms of having to re-do lives, so I kept on searching for my spiritual identity and enlightenment. As I see it, there is no escaping your earth lessons once *you* make the decision to take on your earth suit.

A concept to wrap your brain around has to do with what *free will* may mean to us in terms of eternity. Remember here, that Divine Father has given us "free will." That's a mighty big responsibility. Because with our free will we can make good choices or bad choices. Not a single person is exempt of making choices. It makes sense to me that if we fail "the self-imposed lesson" for one reason or other, that's when we have the choice again to incarnate to try and get it right. This is what my past lives were about and what I was trying to learn for myself. This also explains to me why we are born with a kind of amnesia, which also serves a purpose. As I have promised, I'll go into that purpose later.

For simplicity sake, I've given below a couple of *Webster Dictionary* definitions to save you some time looking them up. Some terms that are misunderstood and need clarification are:

* RESURRECTION: Act of rising from the dead or to rise again. An example that we have all

pretty much heard of before is talked about in the Bible when Jesus rose from the dead.

* **REINCARNATE:** This definition has been distorted and complicated over time, but the original and correct meaning of the word is simply "raise again" or per the definition in *Merriam-Webster's Collegiate Dictionary*: To incarnate again or rebirth in a new body or rebirth of a soul in a new human body. An example would be you-the-spirit taking on a new earth body.

We will get into what this means for a "grown" adult spirit to be born into an infant body.

This is how your God given gifts from another life can show up in the next body—hence musical talent of a grand scale being performed by a three year old, etc. We will talk about the incredible abilities of the Indigo Children being born right now.

* **ASCENSION:** The act or process of ascending; rising or increasing to higher levels, values or degrees. In spiritual terms this simply means you don't die at all; there's no death process involved as we know it, except to say that you no longer have an earth body. So ascension has to do with the movement of spirit. An example would be moving from one dimension to another dimension in spirit form. We presently

reside on earth in the third dimension, but there are the 4th and 5th dimensions and beyond as well.

* INCARNATION: The embodiment of a deity or spirit in some earthly form; invested with bodily and esp. human nature and form. An example would be to give bodily form and substance to a spirit such as ourselves. Simply speaking, "taking on a human body."

* INCURRENT: An entering in or into. Incurrent means to give passage to a current that flows inward. An example would be entrance of spirit into a body.

Chapter 4

What's the big deal about Lessons

IF YOU ARE PAYING CLOSE ATTENTION TO things going on around you, you soon see that there is a lesson in every opportunity good and bad that happens to us. This goes back to why each of us has incarnated—things to learn to do better (love thyself better) and with grace and compassion. Lessons come in all shapes and forms. The late Betty Bethards, renowned mystic and healer, was noted to say in her book, *Be Your Own Guru,* that each of us is here to learn to treat each other with love and compassion. Like I mentioned earlier, she also had a NDE. Betty explains she was raised a fundamentalist Baptist (later turned Methodist) and she believed that when you died you were put in the ground and stayed there until Gabriel blew his horn on the final judgment day. That was until she learned there was no such thing as death. It was when she realized then that one never dies, but changes vibrations, and goes on living and learning on other levels. Betty wasn't convinced that she was supposed to bring her story to the world, until she asked for a sign. Her story goes, she and her husband were sitting in silence, together, meditating and *"suddenly a rush of energy filled the room. I was levitated off the floor."* Her first thoughts were: *"Oh, God, they're going to drop me on my nose!"* But then she says she floated down, and that was sign enough for her.

Indirectly or directly there's no doubt about it—we are here to learn. Lessons are being learned every day. Some painful, some anguishing and always they are life changing or thought rehabilitative.

In my experience the most life-altering lessons are those of Love. Those that follow in importance are showing others Grace. Showing others Compassion. Learning Forgiveness not only for the other person, but a lot of times forgiving oneself.

These, it is my belief, are the magic four lessons at the top of all life experiences. You are the orchestrator and conductor of just how you set these lessons up for yourself.

The other side to this coin called life-lessons are the lessons others are setting up to learn from you. If you don't think it's a set up devised by you and me, look again. Taking one scenario—there's the age old story of love—if you need to learn to respect and esteem yourself you'll find someone who's going to be ugly enough to you to show you how to self-respect and self-love yourself.

These persons are, more frequently than we'd like to admit, the contrast to yourself. How about an old boyfriend. Old girlfriend. Ex-husband. Ex-wife. In-laws.

Bet lessons are happening either to you right now, or to a friend, or to another loved one. Because learning to love yourself as Divine Father loves you is a pretty tough one to learn without the catalyst of help from someone making it painful enough until you eventually stop doing whatever destructive thing you are doing to yourself. If you don't believe being in a painful or destructive relationship is teaching you something, then look closer. The whole point to this life on earth process is to grow us spiritually. Every breath we take and moment we are awake is for the benefit of growing back to our highest spiritual self. We are ever-searching for our original pristine spirit self; the *"us"* without the components of ourselves that we don't esteem. It's like a personal war taking place in and about ourselves. We trap ourselves in bodies designed to improve us or another way to look at it is to elevate us back to our highest place of divinity.

Face it, we are not happy with being who we simply are. If you don't believe me, then why are we always trying to improve upon ourselves. We do this in an outwardly fashion every single day to our natural man bodies.

We are either making ourselves go to school to improve on self, or dieting to improve on ourselves. We make industries of clothing to improve on the looks of our body, industries of medicine to make the body live better, stronger, and longer.

We have makeup and hair industry to help with our body image.

Automobile industry to help improve our mobility to get to the next place better, faster, safer, and let's not forget the look of the automobile because a bright new and shiny vehicle makes us feel happier than maybe our neighbor. We spend trillions on the health industry to improve upon the condition of the body. We go through life doing all the "right" things and rewarding ourselves with this and that material thing made of particles and substances we've put together to improve upon our conditions and circumstances while we are in the body. We have simply forgot who we are, is all. And we are so miserable about it that we are trying to put all sorts of band-aides on us.

The reason we become unhappy, disillusioned, disgusted, hopeless, give-up, and the list goes on, is because we are so busy involving ourselves in daily earth life so we can forget about why we came are here in the first place. After all, it may be easier to face day-to-day on earth than to look inside at the real you.

The real you is just laying-in-wait letting opportunity after opportunity go by to get on with the business of spiritual enlightenment, spiritual improvement, divine identity. Why? The reasons can be as many as the justifications you verbalize as to why you must keep doing the same chasing your tale actions. Money, making a living, raising a family, power, success—are just a few of the distractions that can immobilize that divine part of self you came here to do something about. Now for some of us we realize that there has to be more to life than day-to-day living in an earth suit.

Some of the reason we procrastinate is pure old-fashioned ignorance—you truly don't know who you are, where you came from, and what you're supposed to be doing in the earth suit, other than running around like earth suits hither and yon like everyone else you know. Some of the reason is pure old-fashioned disgust of not knowing what to believe, who to listen to and what to do about what you hear. Ego side of self is great also at procrastinating. Ego dictates—what can be put off today can be done tomorrow.

Some would say then that ego is like a little devil inside your head—making excuses for us.

Keeping us victims of this earth suit we pack around all day with us. Strangely enough, Ego is also to be tolerated with love because it is part of us. That seems a contradiction, doesn't it? A contradiction until you realize we are a living breathing duality of ego and spirit while in our earth suits. Again, it gets back to being Divine Spirit having a human experience. We must learn love and acceptance of ourselves then. Spiritual evolving, enlightenment, ascension comes around to bringing us back to loving and forgiving ourselves for our trespasses to self and others. It's the lesson, you see?

Think about it. All this earth life is about is Lessons to others and ourselves. What we learn. Then life on earth is a school of learning. Ego always likes to make it be about something else, but it really only is a school for spirit to expand upon itself and evolve. I don't know about you, but some day I'd like to graduate this earth-suit incarnation replay of lessons. Stay in spirit form in the Divine realm where every moment is spent basking in a resonance or vibrational constant of peace and love.

This thing called Lessons is tied to our own personal motivation for being here.

Chapter 5

Motivation for Lessons

LET'S TALK ABOUT MOTIVATION (WHY WE HAVE amnesia upon incarnation during human birth and the significance to lessons).

For motivation of lessons to work for us, truly work for us as spiritual beings, we have to have a contrast. Like for instance, the contrast of war to peace. Think about if everything in this earth suit and lifetime were perfect and everything was peaceful—if things were all hunky-dory in our lives—where would be the motivation to make any changes in ourselves—and from our own spiritual point of view—where would be the motivation to spiritually evolve ourselves. Oddly, then, strife makes sense in helping us to spiritually evolve—for motivation grows out of conflict. So as odd an idea or the concept is, war pain then has a purpose in our lives. It makes sense if you see it as a catalyst. If you see you have no death as a spirit. In war you get blown away and you don't die. Just your body does. Does this mean we agree with war? Some of us actually say yes, most of us say no. Is war wrong in our hearts and minds? Are some of us vehemently against war and strive for peace—again some of us agree and some of us don't. Whether we agree or disagree, it doesn't change anything about war having a purpose. However, if you are hung up on the body (the thing you pack around with you everywhere you go) and you think that hunk of meat is all you are and all you have then you are extremely upset about the thought of being blown to bits by gunfire. Being blown to bits, whether right or wrong, provides each and every spirit in human form an opportunity to grow.

I'm talking about everything in life having a purpose, being a catalyst. The people we know are catalysts, the things that happen to us are catalyst to evolve us as spiritual—God created—beings. Take a look at relationships with others, love, war, disease, death—these are all opportunities out of which we learn something.

We learn to love, we learn compassion for someone suffering, caring for someone else besides ourselves, death gets us thinking about dropping our natural body and shifting into spirit realm. We all belong to the college of earth life. We can't escape what we came here to learn. Willing or not, we learn and graduate to the next level whatever that level is.

Think you're putting off the lesson by avoiding the pain or disappointment of something—therein lies the illusion—postponement is merely temporary when you've got a whole eternity in front of you to get the lesson successfully completed. Just knowing this can change your outlook of handling things.

You hear people all the time ask—why is this "thing" happening to me? Well the "thing" has an important function in your personal life, that's why. Now you can choose to drag your feet and spend years learning it, or you can learn to see the pain of it being vital to the growth you predestined for yourself and therefore, confront and get the lesson figured out so you can move on. Why all this fuss about lessons? Because we have degraded ourselves through all kinds of experiences from many different lifetimes and we have gotten ourselves lost. Lost from what? Mostly you've merely lost your spiritual identity. The worst kind of identity theft in the world is forgetting you have first been created in spirit form—you are not the flesh body you pack around. Go to any spiritually-grounded person in the world no matter their race or religion and you will hear the same thing. This isn't my own unique concept or something. This is known knowledge. It is a truth. This truth has a dynamic built in resolution—this truth can and will, if you learn to embrace your true identity, solve all your earthly woes and fears, the fears you face while in your body suit living everyday life on earth. Knowing you are divine spirit brings you the ultimate divine peace. The nature of the kind of peace spoken of in such reverence through the ages that it is no wonder that peace is highest on the resonance scale of spiritual vibration.

Earth life is the just the beginning of understanding the level you are presently at—which is the third dimension.

When you transition to the fourth dimension, you will be transitioning with your spiritual form. The one Divine Father gave us. This is the ancient spirit body—an antique in that it has been around longer than your 50-60-100 year old earth suit.

I know I've given you a whole lot to think about and process.

What you will want to ask yourself here is how long do I go on ignoring my spiritual identity—postponing my identity lesson—living in strife and at effect of the natural world around me? For each of us the understanding of identity and its timing with God is personal. No one can do it for us. No one should take it upon themselves to transform you, command, demand, force or coerce you before your will to learn is ready.

Some of us take years, several lifetimes, and then again if you are born to earth in this lifetime you have a very unique opportunity to finish up what you've got on your plate for the spiritual transition to the next level. Level or dimension, it matters not what you call it. The more learning you have under your belt, the better you become adept at using those terms interchangeably.

Getting back to the amnesia we are born with and to take this one step further—look at how, if we were born knowing what we know on the other side from which we come, it's easy to say we would not be left to our own resources to learn from the motivations moving into our lives. In other words amnesia serves a purpose. We all have to incarnate without having an upper hand so to speak. This means we have to learn by trial and error just like everyone else does.

And when we chose (on the other side) to take on a human body again we had our reasons. The reasons are sometimes simple, sometimes complex, but we still had reasons. Reasons having to do with desiring to elevate/graduate with a higher state of spiritual enlightenment under our belts. Parallel it with why we go to college on earth. To better ourselves. The motivations, again, are many, but you start to see the parallel.

Some of us incarnated to help someone else out with their lessons, and this is the love we exhibit with which Divine Father can see in our endeavors to help each other. I have narrowed it down to three major reasons, there's likely many more you can think of, but I've chosen what I believe to be the top three reasons and the rest kind of align under the three. Betty Bethards was the one whose angel explained to her that before we incarnate from the other side we know what the first 28 years of our lives are going to be like. Then after that, she goes on to explain, we are on our own. This means we have had a glimpse of who we are going to incarnate with or meet on earth to get the job done. Imagine what all this entails and how interlinked we are. Imagine what it means to all be here for one another.

Back to the reasons to incarnate.

First reason to incarnate revolves around learning to love and honor thyself as Divine Father intended when he created us *in His image*. This is where perhaps, like me, you have trouble wrapping the human brain around this truth. Allow yourself a moment—calling on your spiritual brain instead of human one—to embrace the pristine meaning of the concept of what Divine Father is saying. *In His image*—the meaning is pretty clear to a spiritual person.

I knew exactly what these three words meant when bestowed to me. I call it regaining sight of how I started out being this evolved soul before somewhere along the way I stopped believing I was created in God's exact spiritual image and worthy of being perfect in spirit and heart. The Adam and Eve story is one most people have heard of before. With Adam and Eve we are talking about natural man. Our spiritual base, though, is still in God. Adam and Eve were given bodies to go about on earth as natural man and along with their bodies they were given free will to make mistakes. Have you ever known a natural man that hasn't made a mistake? Jesus is exempt here.

He is an elevated spirit come into the natural man form with a very specific and vital mission that transcends earthly defining.

Divine Father created Jesus and Divine Father created us. Divine Father didn't say He created us in a lowered, debase, groveling, pitiful man image.

No. Divine Father created us *IN HIS IMAGE*. And we defile the meaning all to kingdom come and back. We rebuke God when we stray from his literal meaning.

But what else is expected of natural man left to his own self-loathing estimation of himself, but to degrade himself or let someone else degrade him. Because to listen to and accept responsibility for what's been bestowed to us by Divine Father, is a heavy yoke to bear for some of us. If on the other hand you understand your identity and embrace the beauty of your Father's gift to you—being his spiritual offspring—you are set free. Free to have fun with your God-given gifts. Create if you want, manifesting is what some of us call it. Not at all a foreign concept if you embrace your identity. This also goes back to how our thoughts have energy; they have power to create for us exactly what we are thinking. This is another truth, and you know it to be true if you've ever worked with your own divine creative energy.

Second reason to incarnate is to be here as a loving support person for someone who needed to incarnate to clear up something personal with themselves. And yes, this is where you see yourself coming back with loved ones from a past life, so that they can clear up their past regrets or needs. Sometimes you switch places. Mother in past life gets to be daughter in the present life. This is why it is so important to recognize how to apply grace-based parenting. This is where parents need to understand that they aren't dealing with a body who resembles a child, but a spirit that may be wiser and older than they are.

The spirit is just trapped in an infant body, then that body grows. This is why parents have such strife with their teenagers; the parent is either trying to control, manipulate, or talk down to the body of an age-old spirit inside the body. Show respect, kindness, compassion, grace, and listen to what this spirit has to say and you will get a lot further in your parenting.

Another way to look at this through enlightened eyes is to consider that your attempts to protect your child/teenager from harm directly interferes with their own life lessons that they went to a lot of trouble in spirit to set in motion so that they could learn from it in their earth suit. Is it no wonder that some teenagers, living with Ego-driven parents, give their parents such grief in order to get their lessons learned. Now a little aside for parents here: Not to throw your hands up in helplessness; instead of ego interfering, try praying for your child's divine protection. Whatever you do don't have expectations for the outcome. You've maybe heard somewhere in your travels: *Let go and let God*. This is you putting reliance in the spirit world to work things out exactly as divine destiny intended. Too often as spiritual beings having a human experience we get all ego-involved in the loss of someone, or get wrapped up in the human living experience that we forget that the bigger divine force governing us all has taken care of it exactly as it was meant to be. We forget that this human living experience is transitionary. We spend all our human lives fighting against losing bodies, fight against our bodies degenerating, fight against disease, fight this or that, which simply means you have lost touch with your spirit side or spiritual identity and from whence you originated.

Consider for the moment, what if someone who dies at an early age does so because they only needed a short amount of time to either teach their family or learn what they needed to learn and then they get to shed the earth suit and they are done on this side. As strange as the thought may at first appear, if you have trained yourself to see through your spiritual eyes at the broader picture, this is where you start to see that sadly illness and disease have their place in life. The attainment of heaven then is having graduated from life-college on earth and getting to stay in the beauty of spirit form with Divine Father in His special home of elevated wisdom with its eternity of joy and happiness in nirvana land.

If you have trouble remembering from whence you come, just pick up a NDE book.

All the individuals who had these experiences realized while they were in the spirit form on the "other side" that they weren't done or hadn't accomplished all they needed to accomplish on earth and so they returned to their body on earth. In George Ritchie's account, Jesus asked him, *"What did you do with your life?"* George goes on to realize that the question seemed to be a question about values, not facts. Dannion Brinkley had his body zapped twice by lightning and both times his out of body experience (meaning he was pronounced clinically dead two different times by doctors in the hospital where he was taken), encompassed the indescribable love he felt in spirit realm and he realized after talking with Jesus that he had to come back to earth in his crispy and burnt body to finish his purpose, which is to enlighten you and me. You have to understand that Jesus and the Divine realm were not in any way judgmental at all, they simply posed a question to Brinkley about his purpose for the benefit of us all. You have to understand how deeply distressing it is for spirit to have to return to earth after having a glimpse of spirit home again. Their accounts are heartbreaking of the depth of loss they feel, while coming back to their earth bodies, which are usually in bad shape if they have been pronounced dead.

If you think that our earth behaviors put us in disfavor of Divine Father or Jesus, you have to start to see that when Jesus died for our sins, it was a once and for all time act across time and all dimensions. That means He took all judgment and sin upon himself on our behalf for all time. There is no linear time as we know it in spirit realm. Time as we might conceive of it in fact consists in that realm of past, present and future all simultaneously available to us at the same moment. One would think that Dannion Brinkley's profession as a sniper for an Intelligence agency, where he killed others in the line of duty, would have been enough to send him to hell. But you see that the converse is true. Our sin slate was wiped clean by the loving divine act of Jesus. The only thing entrapping us is our own human beliefs on the matter. Divine Father and Jesus realm blows our limited beliefs and judgments out of the water.

If you listen to the bigger picture here, then you see our stages of understanding are just ours. They hold no water in divine spirit home. We do the condemning of ourselves and others. Not Divine Father, nor Jesus, nor any other name you want to attach to them; they show us only the purest unconditional love.

We create, with our own limited belief systems, the hells we are living or going through. Therefore, the blame resides with oneself. So the favor we can do for ourselves is not to project blame out at Divine Father or someone else. It's our own making; we need to take responsibility for our own baggage destiny. No more cop out by blaming someone else. We set it all in motion, with a loving kiss and divine blessing given to us at the door of heaven for our send off to planet earth. So let's grow up and get on with it. Start forgiving yourself for your human experience, forgive yourself and others for the amnesia we are born with and then do something about who you really are.

Dannion Brinkley had to forgive himself, which was probably the hardest job he ever had judging from his story. The accounts of our spiritual and true Divine Father connection in these books is hugely comforting to the rest of us. Which is why Brinkley and the rest came back to tell us about their divine connection stories.

Going back to why we incarnated, think what it means if we know the consequences of what we are doing before we jump into a body on this side in the third dimension. We must take responsibility for our own decisions. Imagine if you will that there is no one to blame for the way we are then. What about being able to blame our parents for everything that goes wrong. Blame God or Jesus for everything that goes wrong or doesn't turn out the way we want. Blame dissolves all around us. You might have guessed that blame is an attribute of Ego. We start to see then, that we are up against ourselves. No one else is out to get us, do us harm that we didn't set up for ourselves, and no one can use the cop-out of making the other person wrong anymore. The pact between you and this other person was predestined by agreements made in spirit. What this does is place you at cause over victim-hood.

Now don't be too quick to judge a person who resides in victim-hood though, as they provide the rest of us an opportunity to cultivate compassion. Looking closer, train yourself then to see that the homeless person living in the streets is there for you just as much as you are there for them. Consider, that they are just as spiritually connected as you and I are by spiritual DNA. Yet outward appearance would invite judgment from a passerby when instead the homeless person's personal sacrifice of comfort to be of service to humankind is to be commended and respected.

They are loved no less by Divine Spirit or God for their humbled role in helping us cultivate our compassion. For all we know we were the one living in the streets the last life time and they were there to show us compassion. This is why, when you start to see through divine eyes, you will notice your spiritual alignment with God sharpening. The way this works, the more you cultivate and tap into your divine connection the more you will notice blessings pouring into your lap. The more you work with your divine sight the more you will filter things with an enlightened eye. The snowball effect of this starts out small, but this vital step will start you looking at things a little differently. Hang in there. At first it may feel awkward, but the more you use this spiritual muscle the better it builds.

Another example to consider: If there were no sickness, no sick and ill or dying loved ones, ill or dying family or friends where would the other group, us caregivers, have anyone to hone in our compassion on. You have heard the saying – it takes two. I can think of no better place to apply that adage than to two people trying to work out their individual lessons they'd come to earth to work out. There is a lot of love and suffering going on for someone at a spiritual level when they have to be cruel.

Consider that it may be at the great cost of one's own heartbreak on a spiritual level, to assist you in learning to love yourself. From an Ego standpoint something that appears insane and an outrage could, from a spiritual point of view, have a very specific divine purpose.

Of course as long as spiritual beings continue to need to cultivate love and compassion and self-love, or evolve themselves, they will incarnate bodies to enable them to overcome chaos and disorder and unexpected and sometimes heartrending events. To keep some semblance of order between one's Ego trying to cancel the other Ego out, on earth there has to be rules and laws imposed—which is merely a means to more lessons to learn. Thus, the cycle goes. Spiritual identity means not missing attachments to things of the material world. If you consider that the human experience is, at best, a fleeting phenomenon, that divine spirit never dies, that you are eternal energy, then things as you see them can fall into place seemingly without effort. Realizing your true identity is liberating—it provides a secure feeling no matter the physical circumstances. Wouldn't it be wonderful to feel that secure?

Third reason to incarnate is to become an enlightened spirit who becomes an inspiring example for all the rest of us to model after.

If you've been paying attention, then you can see from the above example another facet of why Jesus incarnated (aside from absolving us of sin by His death on the cross).

Jesus had such a tremendous impact on us in that we will love and remember Him for eternity. He is our spiritual inspiration that has transcended 2000-plus earth years.

Our job is to not let His tremendous love for us be in vain. We need to carry His torch so everyone can see their way in life.

How can we love thy neighbor as ourselves if we don't love ourselves as Divine Father says we are supposed to? Easy if you see into your neighbor's eyes and recognize God, Jesus, Divine Spirit, is there staring back at you. I've jumped ahead a bit in the book right here. Because it is not always as easy as that until you lay some ground work on yourself.

Chapter 6

Relationships

WHAT DO RELATIONSHIPS DO FOR US? WE have already covered some of this above. Now I'm asking us to get to the meat of the topic. Relationships grow us. That is to say, some of our relationships drag us out of our comfort zones to present us the opportunity to grow spiritually. At the very least we talk about them as being either blessings or curses.

It was many years ago when I was consciously choosing my husband at the time. Or I wasn't so conscious, because back then I was still young and believed in love at first sight or that attraction thing where sparks go off for us when we meet *thee* person we think we are destined to be with the rest of our lives. Wow, I remember thinking I'd like someone tall, dark and handsome. I strangely wanted someone who was the opposite of me—I was this shy and introverted and naïve girl, who really thought of herself as an ugly duckling. While I was shy and introverted and naïve, I was also brave and even courageous, which in hindsight seems a total contradiction. This assessment, though, is what I thought of myself by outward appearances. I have since grown into myself and my values have shifted to what's inside instead.

But back then, my first husband was a high school sweetheart—he was very popular on the JV-Varsity football team, he came from a very friendly and socially outgoing family. I liked his smile and he seemed very interested in me. For a shy, introvert, ugly duckling kind of girl (again, I viewed myself this way), I was on top of the world that Jack (made up name) was paying me attention and we started dating in high school. When we got out of high school it seemed like the next logical choice to move in with him in an apartment. Living together is supposed to give one an idea what kind of person they'd be living with if one married him.

That seems logical. I have to say right here that I had no father figure in my life apart from my grandpa who with my grandma's help raised us five grandkids.

I was the oldest of five, so I had a lot of responsibility put on me, which mostly I didn't mind. Anyway, my father and mother were separated/divorced and I rarely saw my father who had his own separate life.

So to say "any" man paying attention to me was a huge deal is an understatement. Well, Jack and I finally got married after three years.

I didn't realize it back then how vulnerable it made me about my own father not paying attention to me. My grandfather and grandmother did their best to support, feed, clothe us five grandkids, so I didn't think much about how my grandfather didn't seem very involved with us kids. He was also much older than my grandmother, so I think at age 72 he was pretty tired most of the time.

I look back now and realize I chose my parents, and especially my father to incarnate into his life, because he wasn't going to be around or involved in my life. What I didn't know is that I had chosen him since he was going to make me feel I wasn't important enough to him or here's the word, *"worthy"* enough for him to stick around in my life. At the time, of course, I was too young to know I had set this up in spirit realm thanks to the amnesia we are born with.

My high school boyfriend/husband probably treated me too well as I later divorced him (although he was for all appearances headed toward alcoholism). That's when I met the man and married the one who was tall, dark, and handsome and who was going to treat me harshly enough that I'd learn to stick up for myself, respect and love myself. It wasn't until many years later I realize, during my second divorce, that I would not have to incarnate again for the self-love lesson. He had pretty much taken care of helping me to love myself. Of course, back in that day, before my enlightenment as to past-life damaging self-talk, I was blaming John (another made up name) for all my woes, and how unjust he was to me.

It took, not traditional forgiveness toward John as well as myself, but forgiveness of the kind that sticks because radical forgiveness finally made sense.

The author, Collin Tipping and his *Radical Forgiveness* book and his *Radical Manifestation* book hit home for me. The reason it made sense is it explained everything to me as to why the traditional forgiveness was missing the mark. If you have challenges forgiving yourself or anyone else, I find these books incredibly enlightening. Tipping talks about Ego vs Spirit from a wonderful point-of-view as a counselor for cancer victims and his loving spiritual perspective helped me with another turning point in my life.

Dannion Brinkley, author of, *Secrets of the Light: Lessons From Heaven*, also talks about how he learned in his second near death experience how forgiveness holds the greatest consequence for us both on earth and in heaven; and according to Brinkley, "that without forgiveness there can be no ripening of the soul, no authentic way of measuring our spiritual evolution."

I have to agree with them because I finally freed myself with the last step in my spiritual growth being radical forgiveness.

The other upset in my young life was my mother was absent and working out-of-town most of my young life. She was trying, with her parents' help, to provide for five children—again, with no financial help from my father. Maybe you are starting to see how well I set up my earth existence to accomplish my self-love lesson. Needless to say, although we put no label on it as young children, my sisters, brothers and I felt pretty much abandoned. Of course, it was a painful, lonely experience when I let myself dwell on it back then, but on the other hand my grandparents were doing their best to take care of us, so how could I complain.

You see also how I picked my biological parents and my grandparents and siblings for the start of my very necessary growth. And I spent two decades married to John, who taught me what I'd come here to learn.

Funny thing is, when you get your lesson learned and you are healed from your damaging past-life self-talk, you will no longer tolerate the same behaviors from the spouse that you would tolerate before.

It's like living in the dark and suddenly moving into the light.

You won't allow yourself to be disrespected anymore. Even though we had two children together and I was trying to stick it out for their sakes, it was inevitable that we wouldn't stay together.

I can say with hindsight that the moment I started loving and respecting myself, I was making John and myself more miserable by not moving on with life. He's out there now, wonderful blessing that he is, helping the next woman learn to love herself. This is his greatest and most loving gift and sacrifice; what he can do for others. I don't speak of the harshness and labels I used to tag him with—there is no need. I'm no longer bitter or blaming. I was able to leave that relationship with a fresh start to my life.

That road to a fresh start was not, however, without bumps and hairpin curves.

Because, although I had peace, I was strangely still attracting this type of man. Hindsight is wonderful that way. I knew part of the reason I was now attracting a new boyfriend I'll call Bob, had more to do with my nature to see good in all mankind. It wasn't until much later that it dawned on me that I was subconsciously testing myself to make sure I had healed my demeaning pattern of thought where I was not "loving myself enough"; not respecting myself. So all I can figure out, was this religious-minded person I started dating, named Bob, was more a test subject for my whole self-healing graduation.

After Bob moved on with his life, my new journey started. After two decades of marriage followed by multiple dating mishaps, I needed to retrain my pattern of thought anew, which went hand-in-hand with an elevation of my spiritual energy resonance. I'll go into this more in the Divine Energy-Resonance-Vibration chapter. So training myself consisted of reading books on the subject of spirituality, energy vibration, and those that resonated with me I kept reading, those that my spiritual intuition guided me toward I couldn't read enough of. I listened to sacred *I am* music by Jonathan Goldman. I read both volumes of the *Ancient Secret of the Flower of Life* by Drunvalo Melchizedek. I had stacks and stacks of books to read and I seemed to thrive on any subject about self-actualization and spiritual identity.

In college we studied the subject of Erikson's Developmental stages and here I was suddenly approaching the developmental age of Generativity vs. Spirituality. So I was coming into my own, so to speak. This veracious reading frenzy went on for a while, until I started college, and then things became about reading text books on Anatomy and Physiology, Microbiology, Chemistry, and other required subjects related to my degree. Along with college came my efforts toward supporting my daughter and myself. At this time in my life, my son was old enough to have his own life with work and college and we kept in touch mostly by phone. I look back on those insane days of college, work and family and thought I was living as well as can be expected.

Though I was so exhausted at the end of the day from school and hours of study, and taking care of my daughter I still had a few hours on occasion for myself. My soul was starved for spiritually divine connection, so I still tried to read research material for this book while going to school. Glutton that I seemed to be for trying out new relationships, I also tried to date amidst all this. My young adult children were wonderfully supportive and a great blessing to me during this time.

It was only after much insistence from my sister in all her wisdom, that I prepared a vision board. A visual retraining aide is what I now call it. She talked me into making one for myself. So with poster board in hand I started my own vision board. Funny thing is as I started to put some thought into it, I started to look at it in a whole new way. I was actually putting my prayers and wishes onto a board. A whole unexplained phenomena seemed to be unfolding in front of my eyes and suddenly at the top of my board I wrote: "My vision board of things coming to me."

Under that I next wrote the word, "God, followed by Love, Trust, Peace, Compassion, Grace, Kindness, Spiritual, Healed, Healthy, Happiness, and Whole." You'll love this; I have a million dollar bill taped to the board, based on a story told by Jack Canfield, who wrote the *Chicken Soup for the Soul* book.

He had taped a bill to the ceiling of his bedroom so he could look at it every day and affirm his desire. His story goes on to relate that his publisher wrote him a check for the exact amount he had affirmed for himself.

Okay, so I thought what harm is there in wishing for a million dollars. Especially when I could help a lot of people with that kind of money. Anyway, I stood back and looked at my vision board when I had it all done and I remember saying to myself, *"Father God, I wish you could find me someone who is grace-filled and loving and could love me and my daughter without judgment."* I finished my wish with, *"God, how about someone who is a lot like me."*

You've probably guessed it—I'm once again married, but this time there's peace and joy in my life. My husband, Eric (also made up name) and I, share spirituality and peace and friendship as soul mates. Funny thing is my husband never saw himself as spiritual. It was what I saw in him. And I used to tell him that all the time. I used to validate for him that he was wonderfully spiritual and grace-filled and loving. Even when I knew he had gone to Christian college and was raised the traditional religious way, I still re-enforced for him that he was "enough" just the way Divine Father made him. The conversations we have are safe for him to reveal his innermost thoughts and pose his untraditional spiritual questions. We discussed how he had quit Christian College because he had an ego-minded professor who wouldn't allow any student to question his views and opinions. My husband's spiritual vibration complements my own. We can laugh about when we try victim-hood out on each other. We both read pretty much the same materials.

He sees how physics and spirituality can exist together. We both recognize the difference between coming from a place of ego instead of grace and love and spirit. He respects where I'm at spiritually and I respect where he's at spiritually. We frequently get to apply to life the examples of the differences between ego and spirit.

Equally important, he introduced me to a church where the pastors don't call people sinners and the pastors take the time to reveal the original literal meanings of biblical passages for a wonderfully enlightening new look at what Jesus really meant for mankind to know. To fix relationship woes, search out the root of the identity problem in your life. It very rarely has to do with anyone but yourself. It's what you've said or done to yourself that is your yoke to carry around with you. Seek enlightenment, get yourself healed spiritually so you find your peace and joy. Which is what your divine purpose is leading you toward anyway.

Getting back to Spirit vs Ego, remember the mind, heart, and soul of the spiritual identity person mostly resides and operates in love. The mind, heart, and soul of a conflicted and lost soul mostly resides and operates in ego. My experience and teachings have taught me that an ego-based person must feel or be right about everything they think they know, which means, the other person has to be wrong about everything they know. What do you think—each of us have been there and done that, right? We have been in ego mode of operation. We love ourselves for being right if we can get away with it, but it is a false sense of achievement when we have to exploit the other person's weakness or lack of knowledge. We feel pride in making the other person back down and turn tale so-to-speak. These power struggles are base ego behaviors. We have all been guilty of exhibiting the not-so-gracious side of ourselves. Admitting this is considered having a human experience.

The contrast of this, of course by now, you guessed it. Spiritual. This is where we get at the heart of who we really are. The mode of operation of spirit form applies grace and love and compassion to every opportunity that comes our way. This side of us comes from a place of unconditional acceptance. This side of us intuitively comes from a place of understanding in that we are a part of Divine spirit—first and foremost created in the image of Divine Father by Divine Father. We, with our identity in divine spirit figured out, are here for a purpose. Ego-driven divine spirits are also serving mankind, as I have mentioned an example of some of their purposes earlier.

Going back to how Jesus incarnated into body to come and resolve and take upon himself, sin of man for all time. I'm talking about His absolving us of sin in Divine Father's eyes for all time. It was a pure act of love, grace, and compassion. The spiritual person realizes this great act of suffering and compassion came with an eternal absolution from sin, and that conversely, the wide-spread belief of most ego-driven souls deny that He did this blanket act of absolution for us for all eternity. Furthermore, they will insist upon still calling one another sinners, and have so for ages. This is pretty much the accepted norm out there. This type of indoctrination is everywhere you turn. It is well-meant. It is more precisely your belief of what you know at whatever level of spiritual understanding you presently are at. Again, our interpretation of the religious texts hardly do justice to the pristine meaning of the original intent. Again, Jesus, did not write the entire religious texts with His own hand, so what do we expect really to happen. His intent is left vulnerable to limited human interpretation.

I once had a man tell me everything he needed to live by was in the religious text. When I tried to point out that not everything to sustain life was in that text, he argued that yes it was. At this point I should have agreed that this was his personal understanding and his stage of spiritual development was his own. You see, he was not wrong, it was more precisely where his understanding of things was at.

If you try to impose your knowledge on people it only makes them angry. When I tried to explain to the person above that take the food pyramid for example. It tells us that we have to have so *many servings* of dairy, grains, vegetable, fruits and meats. I further explained that this information was not in his religious text, but these servings are deemed essential to support a person's health. When I finally realized he was feeling as though I was trying to make him feel wrong about what he knows, I immediately stopped trying to explain spiritual perspective and I left him to his own stage of spiritual development.

I'm doing a lot of emphasizing, I know. But when talking about Divine Father one can't hear it enough that we each have our own timing with Divine Father. Not that long ago I heard something at a writer's workshop, which put things in wonderful perspective. Wayne Dyer has another wonderful way of putting it. He merely states, "That is your way. This is my way." Very eloquently said, don't you think?

Using Jesus again, as an example, you never hear about Him arguing with anyone.

Not even when He could have argued that some people's perspectives of Him being the son of God or God himself didn't stop us from trying to make Him wrong about who He was so that we could be right and therefore justified in crucifying Him. Jesus really didn't need to give explanations of why He was here or what He was going to do for us. He knew it didn't matter if we believed His story to be truth or not, He knew He would be up against our egos. He was secure in his identity as Divine Christ and He knew what He'd come here for. Jesus with His inherent spiritual knowingness intact and a purpose to fulfill in His earth suit. He knew it pointless to argue…He knew coming here that we each had different stages of spiritual growth and development going on. He knew the egos of humankind, the egos of religion would throw Him to the wolves and deny His existence altogether if they could.

If we simply understand and embrace that our own stages of spiritual development don't make us right or wrong, just makes us aware of where we are at this present time, then no one would have to crucify anyone else. We could be at peace with what we know, when we know it, and that we have an opportunity to know something more or different tomorrow.

My sisters are pretty spiritual in different loving ways. I have a sister, whom I'll call Annetta, and she was burned at the stake in a past life because people of that age were not ready for enlightenment and they feared their own spiritual heritage. But now she has incarnated back into an era in which spirituality is flourishing and expanding.

Our perception muscles are becoming more and more toned to bring us back to our identity. My other sister, whom I'll call Doreen, has no desire at the present to know what her past lives might reveal about her own self-talk programming and no desire to clear that up. Like I said, we are all on our own paths to Divine timing to know things. My sisters and I can get along together because we respect each other for where we are at.

If you are a parent, reinforce for your children that with Divine Father anything is possible. When your children are struggling with a relationship, ask them if they are respecting and loving themselves enough to not subject themselves to the situation. You will have better success in your communications if you try to stay out of the "tell" mode and stay in the "ask" mode, so that they can see how they might think about something.

The way the realization comes from self is better accepted from their own perspective. Remind them that relationships grow them, so that they will always be learning how they feel about something they chose. Try to empower them with validating them about the good choice or decision they made that got them where they are at, and if it wasn't a good choice then you can ask them what they want to do about it. Condemnation in your tone of voice doesn't work for any of us. Leave the censure out of your tone. Children don't have to feel like the victim; they have power to change their circumstances, but the desire has to come from them not what we want for them.

One more time—our children are where they are at spiritually and needing to learn something they desired to learn for themselves. No matter how much we wish we could, we simply can't do it for them.

Chapter 7

Testimony to God is Alive and Well

BECAUSE THE PASSAGES IN THE OLD TESTAMENT and New Testament and all other 900 versions of the Holy Bible happened so many years ago some of us have lost touch with the miracles and with essence of hope. This chapter is devoted to those of you who need to hear that Divine Father is alive and well. Because when we get to hear of a present day miracle it revives us and touches our heart in a new unit of time.

This is vital to hope.

Vital to our lives.

Yes, we need to be reminded on occasion that the unpleasantness of this life we chose is occurring around us to keep us grounded in earth reality for what we have come here to accomplish in our earth suits. But we also need to be spiritually fed. This is as important and vital to us as is food to eat and air to breathe. We must not forget to nurture our spiritual selves or we will feel unfulfilled, lost or even alone. If we neglect our Divine self it will only be for a short while and then something is going to be in your face. It's like ignoring cancer. It will eventually do you in unless you've accessed your true identity and are embracing it.

So I've written this chapter to reeve you up and impart inspiration. These are personal stories of friends and acquaintances. These are not staged for anyone's benefit. I've received permission from the parties to use their stories. To protect my sources, I've changed the names—but these are real life stories of real life people. Ordinary people, like you and me.

I want to remind you here that the longer we live with our eyes open and senses attuned to (even the skeptics of this) and the more enlightened we become the more we start to understand that there are no coincidences. Coincidence is a word the uninformed spirit/soul has adopted to explain the divine happenstances away. Try this; try for the heck of it, if you need to at first, just to imagine the "what if".

Or the possibility that something you said or thought of as merely a coincidence when in essence it is something you're just not perceiving with your divine senses at the moment.

Some of us get this uncanny feeling that "it" has happened before, or when you first meet someone—you get this feeling that you've been there before or you know them.

Suspend for the moment the urge to say it is just some coincidence. Replace the word "coincidence" with "this is divine meaning unfolding in my life". We are beings of this divine realm where we are enacting our earth lessons out. Divine fills all the spaces of our beingness and is all around us and in every living thing and we have access to it because we are created in His image and He is divine. So the divine possibilities are limitless. Again we go back to the verse, *with Divine Father all things are possible.* The more we seek out our true divine identity the closer we get to shedding our self-imposed natural man amnesia and the more we flow with divine sight and divine purpose guiding us. It's like moving on instinct. The more we recapture our divine self the more things you will start to notice about divine happenstances. The more you will see the divine occurrences or call them for what they are—miracles—all around you on a daily basis.

There are some small miracles that occur that we probably gloss right over every time we turn around. So it makes sense that to say that it's easy to notice the bigger miracles that usually get our attention right off the bat because they are showy and stupendous.

I'll let you in on a little secret. The more you start to *expect* to recognize every day miracles as miracles the more fun the divine universe has sending things across your path. It's like living like a child with sparkling eyes wide open and heart unguarded and waiting with breath held for the fairy dust to fall. Look at the face of the Dali Lama and you see the face of a child in constant wonderment of divine possibility in every breath he takes. Every day for him is a wonderland. Get yourself back to your child self. Before earth life battered you around a bit and took the sparkle from your eyes.

Get yourself back to your divine place that is rightfully yours. A place that no one can encroach upon. This is your special sanctuary and a place of nurturing divine self. Run like an excited child toward your divine self and Divine Father will take care of the rest. The more you learn to rely on Him as your sanctuary from the harshness of natural man life the more He smiles His radiant smile and opens His arms wide to embrace you. Run toward your God-given divine identity. There your sanctuary awaits with open arms to receive you.

Now back to the possibilities we each have access to. Keep your eyes open. Think "what if" and await like an expectant child.

One more thing and a big thing worth mentioning—do not await like an expectant child wanting to have your own way, wanting to have the miracle unfold the way you think it should unfold. Instead, train yourself to await the unexpected. Because that is where Divine Father works his magic. Often in ways that stump us when we first see the magic unfolding. Hold onto your chair. I call this the Indiana Jones adventure; you sometimes never see it coming and you always get surprised by the outcome and you may not even see at first how it can be a blessing, but just hold onto your hat and it will be revealed.

I find Divine Father wonderfully humorous with his divine blessings in my life and His gifts and answers are always better than anything I could have come up with for myself and I mean this. Even if I don't see every long reaching angle of it, I have learned to trust it implicitly. I have come to rely on Divine Father for having my back in everything. Heck we have learned we can't trust natural man to have our backs in everything. The muscle we have to build is putting every ounce of trust into the knowingness that Divine Father has our backs every single time. Some readers will understand this place of blind faith and for other readers it will take some effort to reconnect yourself to this stream of divine consciousness.

Don't despair because divine connection is always available to you, it costs nothing but perhaps a few shifts in your perception, and the desire to investigate into your own true identity.

The single most important thing to remember is divine spirit is your heritage, you are and always have been divinely made and you possess already everything you need to start this journey—you come equipped with built in wiring that was Divine Father's making. Your job is to start recognizing yourself for who you are and the miracles you are worthy of receiving or gifting to others no matter how unworthy you think you are, or who you feel you have wronged on earth, or how undeserving you think you are and what havoc or help you have come here to project on yourself or others. This is the unconditional part of the love of your Divine heritage. If you have trouble believing you are loved pure and simply by Divine Father no matter the circumstances you find yourself in here on earth, then you maybe have some influences around you that have been trying to reprogram you and rob you of this divine truth.

Sometimes folks mean well, but are themselves confused about their identity, so beware the well-meaning input that is designed to side track you.

This is where you can be brave and have expectations for yourself that has nothing to do with others agendas and mis-information that is prevalent of natural man. Think of this journey as investing in yourself long term—eternity—this is the depth to which our divine life reaches. We are not the solid mass we see in the mirror, stuck on this temporary stopping ground of earth life and we are not the shell of the withering body we inhabit. I'm sorry if the idea of this is abhorrent to you and goes against everything you currently think you believe in and know. For you, you have all the permission in the world to reject or accept at any time, now or forever anything that does not resonate with you. You are entitled to your free will choice. For the rest of you who seek to reconnect and reattach your divine consciousness to Divine Father flow, feel free to be inspired by the miracles about to revealed in this chapter.

While reading this chapter remind yourself periodically, that *because of our divine connection we are all capable of being miracle facilitators*—I, myself, can maybe make a small contribution to the starting of some miracle happening for you—and so the divine instructions get paid forward as the universe shifts to accommodate our spiritual growth and needs.

John of God, in Brazil, is a miracle facilitator who does both in-person healings and long distance healings as witnessed and received by Dr. Wayne W. Dyer. Dr. Dyer, in his book, *Wishes Fulfilled*, speaks of his own personal healing experience facilitated by John of God.

Dr. William A. Ward, Pastor for 65 years and author of *Miracles That I Have Seen*, is another miracle facilitator who performs on a grand public scale, as well. Ward's book is a 245-page documentary of astounding real life accounts of miracles. He shows us that the trick is *knowing how to speak miracles into existence* and it is simpler than we ever thought possible. Why, as children or adults, weren't we told about this? It's like everything else we have yet to learn. It's because we haven't yet been taught how. Exercising your miracle facilitating muscle isn't something that gets written about in a parenting manual or magazine, so no one expects your parents to know this is something they can teach you.

I've taken just a moment here to give you two examples of miracle facilitators who share with the rest of us their very detailed recipes for accessing our own facilitating muscles. They are not unlike you and me, except that they have figured out how to access their miracle-making muscles.

There are many resources available to you and I've tried to pack this book full of all my own recipes and tools to reconnect you to your divine heritage. In the bibliography at the back of this book, I will list all the references that have helped me arrive where I'm at on my journey to enlightenment. Sometimes all we need is a nudge in the direction—a place to start and someone who has loved us enough to have no agenda apart from simply showing us the tools.

Just like you wouldn't send a carpenter out to build a cabinet without his tools, one must have access to tools and directions found to work by a soul who cares enough to help us get back to our divine spiritual heritage.

Wayne Dyer and Dr. Ward are just two of the many other persons, who tell you exactly how to exercise your divine muscles so that you can tap into your own divine self and your own divine gifts. Skeptics will likely shoot themselves in the foot right here and dismiss this as hogwash, but it takes a braver soul to do the research on self, which is necessary to shed all the untruths that have been fed to us since we were toddlers.

Here's a brief summary of what Pastor, Dr. William A. Ward instructs us to do: "Speak miracles into existence." Dr. Ward says that God showed him that he "has a miracle in his mouth." Instead of praying so much about the problem, Ward was instructed that he could prophesize to the problem in faith. What this means is we must learn that speaking as if the need is in existence as you speak is the divine element that produces the miracle. To summarize; *speaking the miracle into existence is not the same as praying.* Praying is speaking *to* the problem. So retraining ourselves to speak as if God has already put the miracle into place as we form the words is the whole secret.

Dr. Wayne Dyer also goes into the instructions to you and I on how miracles are manifested. Dr. Dyers' way of presenting miracles from a difference angle is wishes fulfilled. I have mentioned in earlier chapters how I have wished from something and it comes true.

Once you start to grasp that all you need to do is realize no matter who you are that Divine Father has your back, that he is happy to be at our beck and call for miracle work, you have it. Remember divine gifts are not just given to some of us and not to others. That is not how Divine Father works. He has given the same gifts to all of us. The difference between us is merely whether or not we know how to tap into our gifts. Whether you know this and accept this truth is not dependent on its existence in your life. That's looking at it the other way around.

Either way it doesn't matter to what is truth. Spiritual DNA is a part of you whether you recognize it or not. Miracles exist whether you recognize them or not. A lot of things go on around us that we are completely oblivious to. They exist in spite of our limited understanding. The spiritual world is in existence in spite of our acceptance of it. Blind faith is all that separates us. The secret to tapping into divine you is just you taking a leap of faith. Adrenaline junkies do this all the time. They just leap. The rest of us are being careful and considering all the angles and rationalizing our way out of the leap. The hurdle we have to overcome then is thinking that we can only rely on and believe in what we see with our human eyes.

What's ironic about all this is a lot of us are going around using our human eyes and ears as a filter. We trust for some odd reason what we see with our human eyes and hear with our human ears. Ironic how once we shed our human senses in body death, we'll have no trouble at all accepting faith, belief, truth, spiritual identity, and so on. Maybe part of the reason we prefer to ignore our spiritual identity is that we live in fear of retaliation from the Divine realm. We are even told by religions of all sorts to fear God. In this case, it's no wonder we turn from our true identity and from Divine Father.

I'm here for the purpose of trying to turn that around. Get us to a place of non-fear.

God, Jesus, Divine Father, whatever we chose to call Him, He is alive and well and contrary to the fear being instilled in us, His home and ours is a dimension of beauty several NDE authors have tried to relate to us with mere words. Divine Father is behind us even when we are insistent on using the seeing-is-believing filter.

As I promised, at long last, here is a sampling of testimonies to our "Divine Father is alive and well":

I PRAYED FOR HELP FOR MY DAUGHTER

I was in college and also working two days a week and in those days I was balancing school, mountains of homework and taking care of my daughter. I remember I used to say all the time, the only thing getting me through college was the grace of God and my dearest friends who all helped me and wanted to see me succeed. I also remember praying and wishing with all my heart one night that I had the money to get my daughter the medical care she needed.

I had class early the next morning, so sleep was vital.

I also cried myself to sleep that particular night. The next morning as I drove up to the double doors of the community college I was attending, waiting for me outside the doors to class stood a dear friend and classmate Sally. We greeted each other with hugs. That's when Sally handed me an envelope and told me that her mother would want me to have "this" for my daughter. In surprise and total bafflement, I opened the envelope and peered inside. It was a cashier's check. I looked up at my friend with tears blurring my vision and rolling down my face. I sagged against Sally as I felt like I might drop to my knees in speechless gratitude. We both cried and held onto each other for a long time. I somehow managed to speak around my tears and told Sally that I had cried myself to sleep last night as I prayed for help for my daughter. That's when Sally explained that even though her mother had passed away, Sally felt a strong feeling that her mother wanted her to share a portion of her inheritance with my daughter. Sally was convinced her mother wanted my daughter to have the gift. I knew it—knew Divine Father had divined a miracle for my daughter. I was able to get the medical help my daughter needed. I always told my close friends and family about the circumstances when witnessing miracles in my life. I told them about the miracles to give them hope and give glory to Divine Father.

I WIN LOTTO MONEY

I had just heard of the movie, *The Secret*, from my sister who called to tell me she was sending it to me and was insisting I watch it. My sister whom I've talked about earlier is a very spiritual soul and was really excited by what she saw on the movie, so I told her I would watch it as soon as I received it. For any spiritually secure person (notice I did not say religious person) the parallels I saw in the movie with Divine intervention is very apparent to me. I have since had religious friends argue the point with me, but non-the-less I saw the intervention of Divine Father all through the message and what the author was trying to teach us. I had to watch the movie a couple of times to wrap my brain around the concept and own it. Of course, like millions of viewers, I earnestly paid attention and implemented the exercises Rhonda Byrne walked us through. Since I know Divine Father is involved in everything connected to us (his children on earth), I had no doubts that God was intimately involved in this knowledge that she was imparting to us. So I paid close attention.

After about a week of absorbing the material and practicing like she instructed, I got a wonderful acknowledgment and affirmation of the far-reaching effects of God's delight in us. I had bought a lotto ticket. I had not chosen any of the numbers myself. I let the machine pick them for me. To my way of thinking, I would let God have total control. It was more fun for me to wait for Him to surprise me in His own way.

You have to understand I was always delinquent in getting back to the store to get the winning numbers, but this time I was a little more excited and it only took me a week to follow up—ha-ha. I was at the convenience store and heard the whirr of the machine and the cashier looked up from the ticket this time to announce "you just won $400.00." You would have thought I won a million dollars for all my hooting and hollering and jumping up and down I did. I immediately accepted my monetary affirmation of

Divine intervention in my life and smiling like a child in a candy shop, I walked out of the store, called my family and friends to attest to the Divine power of belief and law of attraction in my life. I imagined Divine Father smiling and hooting and hollering for me, as well. I also profusely thanked Divine Father. Gratitude is a huge factor in this Divine consciousness life I lead.

NO MORE HEADACHES

Brian said that when he was working his job in drafting, one of the things he was told was that he would get a lot of headaches. The headaches in this line of work are caused by intensely concentrating and focusing on the places where the point of the pencil lead meets the paper. Brian explained that he prayed to the Lord that he wouldn't get headaches and the Lord indeed took away the headaches. Brian says, "To this day I don't get headaches. I can even bump my head and I still don't get headaches."

OBTAINED AGENT FOR BOOK

I remember sitting down one evening and did meditation and affirmation to bring the "Perfect Agent" into my life. This was back when I wrote women's fiction and the market was a bear to break into. Anyway, I kept up the meditation and affirmation exercises with heart-felt intensity for nearly two weeks and then one day I received an email from R. B. who was an agent who believed in my story.

I thought I would be able to market it to the publishers she knew. R. B. turned out to be my perfect agent.

※

BOUGHT A HOUSE ON A HANDSHAKE

Tom explained how his wife, Nancy, had prayed for their house to come into their lives. After about a week and a half of Nancy praying fervently for their house to show up, the couple went out looking again for the home to fit their family of four. Nancy says they drove up a street and saw that the For-Sale sign had been taken down on a home that had been on a listing three months back. The house from the outside looked perfect, but there was no For-sale sign. Tom and Nancy decided to knock at the door to see if anyone was home. The owner, Bill, was home and invited them in. Bill told Nancy and Tom he had taken the house off the market because he and his wife had decided not to sell. Oddly enough, Nancy says, that Bill ended up showing her and Tom through the house. The more Nancy, Tom and Bill visited and talked the more the house "felt" right for them.

Nancy and Tom would never have guessed that the owner would still be entertaining the idea of selling and Bill seemed to like Nancy and Tom. Bill said he and his wife had been toying with the idea of putting the house back on the market, but hadn't gone to a new realtor yet. Everything seemed to flow so effortlessly, Nancy said, from there on out. Bill called his wife and his wife gave him the okay over the phone to sell the house to Nancy and Tom. Nancy and Tom couldn't believe their prayer had been answered that soon, and the strangest thing was that Bill sold Nancy and Tom the house on a handshake, which was never done in this day and age. The financing and sale went smoothly, which Nancy said was a sign to her that God wanted them to have the house that didn't have a For-Sale sign up.

※

NEED MORE HOURS AT WORK

I remember feeling a bit of anxiety about not having enough shifts at work, which would impact my take home pay. That was back when I was a single mom and I had to have 80 hours a pay period to cover rent and all the other bills. Every month, I would get the schedule for the whole month and then go home to look it over and find out I was short a day or two. I would remind myself to just relax as I immediately appealed to Divine Father, *"Please help me Father. I need more work."*

Sometimes I say this aloud and then sometimes I merely feel and think it. It was uncanny how fast Divine Father would work. Within the hour, I got a phone call from the scheduler saying so-and-so couldn't work a particular day, which I happened to have open. By Father's design, I would get enough hours. This kind of rescue by Divine Father happens to me all the time. I will passionately ask Divine Father for help and the universe will shift things around for my rescue. I will always be just as quick to show gratitude and thank Father for His help. I ask for help with total faith in Divine Father. It's kind of like I said earlier in this book, *"I know He has my back and is always happy to help me when I ask for help."* I also, always leave the outcome of the solution completely up to Divine Father. I have come to learn that miracles come in all shapes and forms and not all of them have to be grandiose to be meaningful miracles.

I remember another time, only a hand-full of months ago, when I didn't even worry about the work schedule. This particular time I noticed that two pay periods were short about 8 hours each. At this time I just took comfort in the fact that if that's the way the schedule is supposed to turn out then I should just be content with what I have. I *"knew"* Father was taking care of me and that I had nothing to worry about. Well, it was a Divine shift in the universe again. This time, low and behold, one of the other employees approached me out of the clear blue and said she noticed I was short some hours, and she offered to share her hours with me! That kind act of Divine love on part of the other employee was just another way Divine Father is working in the gap between us—He was showing us both that He knew the desires of our hearts and it was a true blessing for which I was so very grateful.

MEDITATION MIRACLE

My husband and I have been meditating and anointing by the Lisa Keyes methodology and have found great spiritual breakthrough. The calmness of our life every day following the start of this daily anointing ceremony and meditation is a miracle of peace for our household.

This is testimony that my husband is evolved from his old place of existence to his divine higher-self realm.

Money matters that would have normally been having him pulling his hair out and stressing have completely melted away from our life. The vibrational realm into which we have shifted has been a phenomenal breakthrough thanks to Lisa's gentle and loving tutelage. We have so much to be thankful to Lisa for, grateful for her wisdom and assistance in expanding ourselves into the divine realm of love, peace, and joy. *Namaste.* Which means, *"I acknowledge the divinity in you."*

TRAFFIC TICKET WON'T PRINT OUT

I pray for protection for my kids all the time. I don't have any doubts that Divine Father and their Guardian Angels are looking after them. This story is proof to me. It's kind of an embarrassing thing to admit, but this was such a great example of God's protection, I couldn't leave it out. My daughter called and left me a message on my phone because I couldn't answer the call—I was in a job interview. Anyway, when I called her back she proceeds to tell me she got pulled over for speeding in a residential zone. Anyway, the officer goes through all the routine with her and my daughter doesn't try to ask for grace and see if he would just give her a warning. She fully expects him to give her a ticket. Anyway, I have to say right here, no one on the road or otherwise was exposed to any danger by my daughter's excess speed. Well, you've probably guessed it. The Officer came back to stand at the window of my daughter's car and proceeds to tell her that it had to be her *"lucky"* day, because he had given out eight tickets that day already, but for some reason, in his words, *"the printer in my car seems to like your ID and will not print out a ticket for you."* The Officer said he tried several times and couldn't get it to work. This is after he's been giving tickets out all day prior to this. Now this type of thing may seem coincidental or something, but the fact is, she seemed to be protected even from that type of encounter. Even if the Officer was making it up, or the machine had run out of paper, which is a possibility, the fact is my daughter seemed to have God's favour no matter how you look at it.

To summarize—I live a life of welcoming Divine Father to intervene wherever He sees fit.

I go with *His flow* and when it's *His flow* it feels effortless and then I know in my heart that this is the *God way* in which I need to allow myself to just float.

I also, thank Father with all my heart for His steadfast grace and love. He is my Hero. My very dearest friend. My world. My souls' peace.

Remember here that I'm not a religious soul. I'm a spiritual soul. I think it's important to understand that I don't have to be reading the Bible or going to Church to be loved and taken care of by Divine Father.

Please understand I'm not saying that reading the Bible and going to Church doesn't work for those people who choose that route to Divine Father. What I am saying, is that we each have our own way of perceiving Divine Father, and we can each have our own personal timing with Divine Father and he doesn't reject me because I'm not a Bible reader. Father loves me for being unique in myself and for my being a spiritual soul. Again, I fearlessly proclaim that

Divine Father is the Father of all mankind—not excluding any of us for having our flaws and our own unique Divine timing.

I say—be respectful of others and their own Divine timing.

We are where we are in our spiritual development. Don't make someone else feel their way is wrong just so you can be right. Practice grace and acceptance and unconditional love.

If someone is giving you a hard time about your own personal beliefs, just tell them like Dr. Wayne Dyer tells them, *"That is your way. This is my way."* End of discussion.

Note For the Lottery to be won: From a *Slice of Pi*, by Liz Strachan pgs. 47 & 48. *"To work out the chance of getting all six winning numbers from the possible forty-nine numbers you work out 49C6. Which all cancels down nicely to (49x48x47x46x45x44) divided by 720, giving 13,983,816. So the chance of winning the jackpot is roughly 1 in 14 million."*

To me this represents Divine Father working a miracle for all of the winners of the Lottery.

Chapter 8

Spirituality vs. Religiousness

THIS IS WHERE I SPEAK FRANKLY ABOUT what is a healthy "identity with God" perspective and what is ego-driven perspective. This is where you will want to grant grace to the other person. I'm not judging, remember this. It doesn't make anyone wrong or right either. Remember we, you and I, are entitled to our own perspective of Divine Father, and that our perspective should be respected for spiritually we are where we are at any given time. Just remember, if the person representing God is coming from an Ego-driven perspective then they will want you to feel wrong about what you think so they can be right.

I think we have all seen throughout history that this can be carried to extremes; I'm talking fanatics of any belief. The most healthy thing we can do for all involved is show this person acceptance and love. Because they have a right to their perspective of

God. James Twyman, author of *The Moses Code*, sums up Spiritual vs. Religious by giving some contrasts to look at. Into the contrast and comparison arena, according to Twyman, religious people will look for God somewhere other than in themselves. Religious people also think, just as Betty Bethards originally thought, that one must die to get to heaven, while the spiritually awakened individuals understand that the kingdom of God is within and I take it one step further to include that He is all around us, as He is within us.

I explained it like this once. Imagine Divine Father's essence as a blanket laid down upon the earth to wrap every tiny nook and cranny with His Divine essence so that every fiber of every living cell is enveloped and permeated with Divine Father's DNA. For the last point of contrast, Twyman goes on to say that, *"Religious people sometimes state that God is holy and they are not," where the rest of us spiritually-minded have embraced our Divine identity and become one with the Holy Spirit.* See how this is a matter of personal perspective.

The biggest contrast is the view on God's love being portrayed as conditional, by words coming out of human mouths, whereas, those of us of a spiritual-mind know that there is only unconditional love bestowed us for the duration of earth life and life beyond. These are very interesting differences in perceptions as we hold onto our beliefs for dear life.

Do we realize what we are costing each other in energy, to defend our mere perceptions?

Would it not be better for us to join efforts in spending our divine energies for a cause that has nothing to do with strife and everything to do with care and love of one another?

What about the perspectives that are designed to drag you down, get you off track with your spiritual identity, and make you feel bad about yourself? What can we possibly hope to accomplish with this unhealthy approach to one another? This is where, mentally and verbally if I have to, I will always say to myself "cancel, cancel", which is a trick I learned from Betty Bethards to shield anyone else's words sticking to me when I know they aren't true. It's a lot like editing what you hear. Which I will go into later as this is the bulk of why I had to incarnate over and over before clearing up the negative beliefs about myself. So you can see here why I'm passionate about what I take to heart for myself. Why I have to say "cancel, cancel" both silently and aloud when it's needed. I've even shocked myself and spoken up for someone else who needed a "cancel, cancel" said on their behalf.

It bears repeating. If you find yourself feeling worse about yourself, being told you are just a sinner is a huge negative cloud of untruth—then you have now the tool to buffer yourself by merely saying, "cancel, cancel." I will say from personal observation that a lot of us have had need of this buffer on more than a huge number of occasions—depending upon one's physical body age. Of course, by just excusing yourself from the situation you can also save yourself a lot of strife.

Trying to explain to them, that they are just at some stage or another of spirituality, that where each of us are at is on God's timing and not man's timing, is not what most people want to hear.

The Ego prefers that you are recruited to Ego's way of thinking.

I've spent 40 years of my life searching for truths—I know what it has cost me, the obstacles, the tears, and the relationships. For me, every time now that I hear someone claim I'm a sinner I quickly tell myself to cancel those harmful things out, that Divine Father is the only one whose opinion matters in the end and He's not telling me I am the horrible things someone's ego is trying to attach to me. Not until my present husband introduced me to a different kind of pastor, did I start to hear the truths that resonated with the essence of who I am. Not until then, did I find hope and was I able to write this chapter.

Whatever it may be that has gotten you to where you are looking at the start to spiritual enlightenment, you can give immense thanks.

After a long and diligent four-decade search, I have been shown a home of worship, where God's true meaning of things in the Bible is blowing me away. The reason it is blowing me away is because it is more aligned with what I've somehow sensed all along. I can't help but feel I can't be the only one who has ever been faced with this dilemma. I wonder how many of you have been holding out from going to a house of worship because you were wary of what you would hear and have to face.

Again, I will insert here—respect the person for where they are at spiritually. If they can't afford you the same respect for where you are at spiritually, so be it. As egos' go, it's sometimes hard to admit there's been a mistake, harder still to admit to oneself that what we thought of as truths have been altered perspectives of what is right under our noses. Even what I know today will shift as I'm expecting it to. My quest for knowledge is never-ending and I like it that way.

For most of us even after we have overturned one rock of discovery, low and behold there is another rock ahead of us in the path to overturn.

This spiritual road is ever-evolving, ever shape-shifting and constantly taking on new aspects while discarding others.

The trick is to keep abreast of information to wade through for nuggets of precious truths. Natural man has been guilty of distorting truths as long as we have been incarnating. Our brains can alter things and accept them as truths especially when we allow others to tell us falsehoods without questioning or cancelling them out. This is the human experience factor we are up against. You try to point out one person on earth who hasn't made a mistake in perspective or perception and I'll show you a perfect world in which everything is spiritually-oriented. It's no wonder that perceptions can alter.

It's like this; about 20 years ago I was told to stare at this new kind of picture; many of us will remember these pictures. They hung all over the place, doctor's offices, at work, at home; and if you stared at them long enough (we were told by our friends or co-workers) that we would see another shape take form behind the picture that was readily visible. So I spent countless minutes doing this each day, until one day I finally saw it—the eagle flying in the sky. The three-dimension picture held an image behind the one that was apparent to all passersby. Spiritual beings having a human experience see life like this. And we have to train ourselves to see otherwise—see what is *really* there.

Like I explained in chapter one how we don't see so much of the world going on because we are trying to perceive it within the limits of the five senses. Then we add the human ego factor in the mix to try and make sense of things and therein lies the possibility for error. Our brains are designed to search for earlier similar experiences or pictures and when we come up with no readily available earlier reference it confounds us.

Like I've said, humans like orderliness—things in an orderly, black and white manner. Concepts outside this orderly reference make us short-circuit so to speak.

Fear is at the root of all misconceptions and mistakes and problems with reality. Knowledge, however, replaces fear. The trick is finding accurate knowledge.

Many things in life are like this. We have to retrain ourselves. To see. Without distortions. To think the spirit way. To hear and see truths and not blindly believe what we are told. For instance, you should read not only this book, but others by other authors, and then use all the data to compile your very own truths. There's an old saying in the Fiction writer's world—find three references that hold the same opinion and you stand a good chance at the authenticity of the research—or so the industry says since we are going to use the research to write our own book.

Apart from that, all the wise people of the ages will tell you to take what intuitively feels right and chuck the rest. This is mostly correct. The other aspect of this is that sometimes we are not ready to see and hear in the unit of time that it is presented. What feels right, is always dependent upon what new knowledge you have incorporated and digested. It is dependent upon whether you are ready for the knowledge.

Being ready is a huge spiritual common denominator. If we are wrong about something we can allow ourselves grace in understanding that every law in the universe of physical and spiritual matter is governed by timing. I call it God's timing. Others may call it something else. But once you get this concept you will be able to rely on it in everyday life. If your timing with the subject is right, you will be able to see and use it. All our timing on earth has a built in God-timing factor. Something you don't know today—not a problem—you will one day be ready to know it. In this universal truth we all grant each other grace, by not unjustly placing our expectations on others. By not placing demands on each other that serve our own egos.

I once heard my pediatrician tell another mother to stop worrying about having her child potty trained by age three. When she looked at him blankly, he merely pointed out, "have you ever seen an adult not potty trained." The answer is no.

In this little example, you start to see that not everything has to be according to man's idea of timing.

We would do better in our dealings with one another if we just relaxed and let go of our *"must have it my way"* attitude or I must have it on my terms.

Those of a more religious bent, who usually insist there's no other way to look at things and everything needing to be black and white—well they can pass through our lives with us granting grace to them—that they are still capable of growth just as I am and their fixed ideas will one day undergo a transformation when they are ready just as my ideas will one day undergo another transformation when I'm ready. Some will take their ideas to the grave. So what. It's their choice. They simply had a different idea of the timing than you did. It doesn't make either of you wrong. That's the way God's grace is designed.

If we go through life trying to impose our beliefs and ideas onto others, it causes nothing but resentment. Nothing is learned by pressing a person to learn when they aren't ready. They won't be glad. It will be drudgery and cause ill feelings. Stop imposing. Start allowing things to work out in their own timing. Considerations on time becomes a human thing when we take on an earth suit.

In the fourth dimension where we are once again in spirit form there is no such thing as linear time. In that realm if you can imagine it at all, you experience past, present and future simultaneously. Different universal laws of spiritual abilities apply to different realms. We have a hard time wrapping our heads around this because we have been so far removed from our natural heritage of spiritual being.

Chapter 9

God Indoctrination

MY HUSBAND IS ONE OF THOSE HUMAN beings who is truly worthy of being labeled pure of heart with God—his demonstration of unconditional love is quite extraordinary as a follower of traditional faith goes. He demonstrates friendship at its best. To recognize and accept that I have in some ways outgrown the necessity of belonging to a worship following, is a strange place to be. That is to say, I am free by God's design, to have a free will view of my own. I don't need to copy-cat or mimic behaviors that are popular with any particular group and yet we are all interrelated by our Divine DNA.

If we are being truthful with ourselves, we are trying to conserve, protect and defend God's intent, but we are only capable of doing a mediocre job at best. We have parchment that is organic and chemically breaks down. We have ink that fades over time.

We live in a world that erodes and deteriorates as it was designed by Divine Father to do. The only true preservation of Divine Father is what He imprinted on our hearts as His spiritual offspring. No one can take that from us.

This should be the most universal lesson of all—that we cast no stones. For surely they may be cast back at us on down the road.

In the lineage of 2000-plus years language has expanded and morphed. Intent, inflection of voice, meanings of words have been lost or replaced, or missed entirely by humans who have spiritual amnesia. So let us not sit in judgment of one another spiritually, when our limited understanding of spiritual life in a physical world makes us all vulnerable. Judgment of humans—of human behavior—how do we not fall into the trap of judgment of one another? The answer, I sense, is we cultivate Grace. If you think you are judgmental or been told you are judgmental or legalistic or any other negative label then perhaps you could cultivate a bit more Grace.

Read as many books as you can find on the shelves from people who know what grace is and means and learn how it can transform your everyday life. Applying grace to life and circumstances will feel foreign and strange and out of character at first, but if we learned anything from Jesus we have learned what grace looks like when we are dealing with people.

If someone is boohooing your application of grace and putting you down for using grace in your life to deal with others, you know that person still has much to learn about grace as well.

It is not something taught in traditional schools, grace is not perhaps something practiced by most parents, so you get no training on how to apply grace until you do your own research. Remember, I mentioned the importance of grace. It is another lesson most of us can easily miss, but I believe it is something we could learn to cultivate in order to evolve ourselves into a higher spiritual vibration.

When you consider how we like to control things, we have to have tools to help us transcend and resonate in a tone that allows the greatest shift in our vibration. As humans trying to survive this earth experience, we seem to be happiest trying to control things. Control others. Control environment. Control, control, control, so unless we are grounded in our spiritual identity we are more likely to make unhealthy decisions, even detrimental decisions with an imperfect perception. The worst part is, unless you evolve yourself, you will operate out of predominately your Ego. So if you are mostly operating out of Ego as an absolute authority who thinks things must and will be your way or the highway, you will be missing your chance to evolve.

My imagination here sees God shaking his head and sad that we are getting all hung up on and detracted from His base teachings of unconditional love, acceptance, forgiveness and grace.

When we take a holier than thou stand, that is we let Ego dictate, we need to remember our measuring stick alerting us to our own foolish stubbornness. Remember the trick to evolving is tied to communicating with grace, love, and acceptance while respecting the other individual for their place and pace of spiritual knowledge.

It bears saying again—that all any of us have to do in the face of conflict, worry, and getting defensive is to remind ourselves we are spiritual beings. Being spiritual we can let go and let God. The transformation that follows is a miracle of its own. If you have no skill or experience at letting go and letting God, then you can ask Him to help you. Faith is knowing that Divine Father has already answered your call for help. If you are watching closely you will be able to see that Divine Father is instantaneous. And the more you are watching closely the more fun He has with sending you blessing, after blessing, after blessing.

For all of natural man's flawed endeavors, the Bible is usually the first reference someone will direct you to for a great tool to the start of knowing God. Look forward to relationships that provide opportunity for spiritual growth. While still in the fledgling stages of spiritual growth it also bears saying, be aware of where your vulnerabilities lie. Pay attention to who's coming onto your path and remember any person with contention in their voice or behavior are probably not going to be coming from a place of being healthy spiritually. They are not necessarily the spiritual person you want to look up to. Because we are all at different spiritual vibrations, and all have a lot of work to do on ourselves in the area of unconditional love, compassion, acceptance, grace, and forgiveness—we can only truly be a therapeutic contact in carrying out Divine Father's work when we have no ego agenda or have managed to be at peace with our duality of ego and spirit.

It bears reminding yourself all the time—put a visual reminder on the bathroom mirror, on your bedroom ceiling, or anywhere else you tend to look—remind yourself, if you need to, that knowing Divine Father is a continual journey and each of us are on that journey at different levels of enlightenment and knowledge. I will say, beware, that our growth in knowing Divine Father can be stunted. What I described above are people getting discouraged by painful encounters with those who know only about black and white. It bears repeating. In my experience God is also all about the gray areas. His gray areas are a test to see if we are paying attention or just stagnating.

You don't have to make this about who needs to admit they are wrong and who's right. God is not about ego. God is about showing loving respect for each other. Good, bad, ugly we must look beyond the visual of it and embrace with our hearts. We are to learn how to do this no matter the circumstances. Yeah we all know this, right? When we can pull off the unconditional love, forgiveness, and grace we must share with one another which is our Divine calling as offspring of Divine Father, then what do you want to be doing when you no longer need to come back to earth with amnesia and keep trying to do it right? I don't know about you, but I'd like to retire from incarnation and just hang out with Divine Father, or as close as I can be to Him.

My fascination with life is to conduct my actions and behaviors to make Divine Father smile. What he wants for us to get—is we must learn to honor and love thyself as He loves and honors us.

At the time I was writing this chapter, I had been going to this church for four months. That's all the longer it took to recognize I was in the right place at last. The logo of this church is, Welcome Home. Rather pertinent to me. Father's House Ministries can, using literal definitions, clear up the misinterpretations using the Bible everyone else uses to shed light on Divine Father for you if you don't find you're yet ready for the spiritual-minded realm and yet you find yourself weary of the path you've been walking. More can be found at fathershousefc.com.

Chapter 10

The Blending of Science & Divine Father

THE MARRIAGE OF SCIENCE AND DIVINE FATHER can be observed as Vibration, Resonance, Light Energy—blending our Divine DNA and Quantum Physics. It has taken thousands of years for scientists to evolve to the point of Quantum Physics—I think it's interesting that Scientists have just named a particle *The God Particle*. See more about this in Appendix A.

Not until I started delving into Sacred Geometry as explained by Drunvalo Melchizedek with his Quantum Physics mind and loving heart, did the parallel universe of Science and God start to blend for me—to make sense. Then I remember all the reading I've done and the research I've done over the years and the time it has taken to piece it all together in a cohesive example of how we are Divinely created to work with this divine stuff.

There are so many overlapping parallels on the blending of science and spirit—*Healing Light* by Larry Lytle, a Doctor who wrote the book and developed the QLazer device (soft laser therapy) and his research on healing at a quantum, cellular level—with FDA approval for Osteoarthritis and Carpal Tunnel. One of the many protocols he offers is a special section on Chakra Balancing with the QLaser. This author believes that benefits are more closely connected to combining wavelengths in such a way to form Soliton waves, which can penetrate the body with resonating quality, and have exact control of power density and frequency. He points out that it is only recently that computers became small and sophisticated enough to accomplish this feat. We are talking about energy vibration here.

Remember we are born into this very special time—if you are here on this planet in body form you have arrived with the rest of us on a very special mission as I will expand upon with the ascension discussion coming up next.

Quantum Touch by Richard Gordon, another researcher and healer who teaches special breathing and body focusing techniques to raise your energy level so high that with light touch you can see postural corrections spontaneously occur as bones gently glide back into correct alignment. He has performed this in front of live audiences.

The Intention Experiment by Lynne McTaggart, who draws on findings of leading scientists from around the world to demonstrate that thought is a thing that affects other things and offers the reader to take an active part in its original studies using cutting-edge research conducted at Princeton, MIT, Stanford, and many other prestigious universities and laboratories.

Her book reveals that the universe is connected by a vast quantum energy field.

You start to see a theme here with energy and vibration.

Qigong (pronounced chee gung) by Garri Garripoli, who studied under a renowned master of Eastern healing techniques teaches us how to understand Qi (our bioelectric life force) to heal ourselves and others.

Again, God has built within us all this divine life force energy as part of our spiritual DNA. All these elements talked about are part of our DNA makeup—our divine fabric, which forms us—our Oneness with Divine Father. What I've learned from Drunvalo Melchizedek in his volumes 1 and 2 of *The Ancient Secret of The Flower of Life* is that I'm an energy body—Light-body. For me, the more I learned about Sacred Geometry the more my awareness expanded to encompass sacred DNA and how divinely I'm made within the Divinity of the universe—my Star

Tetrahedron shaped energy field that surrounds my human body—God made.

Drunvalo Mechizedek is so very lovingly thorough in his descriptions of us as light bodies—it was revealed to me, as the universe's supply and demand equation is so accommodating of me, that I found that within 20 miles of where I live a beautiful spirit person was awaiting to activate my Mer-Ka-Ba light field.

I was able to find Marsha Hankins in the magazine I always pick up from the Health food store I go to for supplements. There within the pages, as soon as I saw the words Mer-Ka-Ba, I knew the information was divinely put there for me to find—it's like opening a cookie jar to look inside to discover the whole universe awaiting. Needless to say I didn't hesitate in contacting her. Learn more about Marsha at iamstandinginthelight.com.

About a week later, I found myself and another person attending the activation session. The other lady participating in the exercise was a Reiki energy practitioner. We started out with our energy field out about seven or eight feet—this was measured with a divining rod.

When we were done with the activation of our Mer-Ka-Ba, our energy fields measured 70 feet out—we had to go outside to measure the length with the instrument Marsha held. From that point on—I could *feel* my energy swirling in motion around my human body. Feeling it always brings a smile to my face. On a deep soul level I feel like I have reconnected with a dormant part of myself and it is a joyful occasion for me. Sometimes, when I just let go of control of my energy field, my body will actually start to sway in a tiny, nearly imperceptible way, in a back and forth fashion from the swirl of energy. My husband always gets a kick out of this when I bring it to his attention—of course we had conversations about my reasons for activating my lightbody—and he never felt he needed to do the same thing. This is part of the respect we hold for each other being on our own individual timing with Divine Father teachings and growth. We don't make it about being right or wrong about something we know—it's more about each of us being where we are at spiritually. There's my way and there's my husband's way—we live harmoniously with that truth. We both understand there is no place in God's world for judgment of each other.

In the movie that came out, *Now You See Me*—at the end of the movie you get introduced to the *Left Eye of Horus*. Melchizedek has a whole chapter devoted to this mystery school.

Melchizedek has our sacred geometry spelled out for us. He has all the scientific ratios within his teachings to us that align *"the size of the Earth being in harmonics with (in phi ratio to) the Moon, and these ratios are found in the proportions of our human energy fields and even in the very Egg of Life itself."* You see in his volumes how closely the marriage between science and divine self—how we are all Divinely created. Nice, huh.

Because the concept of *"God created science and thus the universe"* is something I had to wrap my brain around and Melchizedek's documentation and research was new to me, and I was trying to absorb so much of his material as fast as I could, it didn't at first hit me. It's one of those thoughts that start out in an abstract parallel and eventually blossom into a merging of two. It's like the more you pay attention to what is being said about both, the more sense it will make. This is where you have to open your eyes and mind to something new. Not an easy task by any means since I've beaten you over the head now about how humans like it all black and white.

Not an easy task to keep your eyes and mind open to new data because one has to learn how to suspend disbelief—in order to get to the truth. And then I tell you our truth can take on new dimensions all the time—every day if we are keeping our eyes open. Kind of like when we had to finally accept the truth about the world being round, after we had been told it was flat—from there we even learned we had a universe around us.

Unexplored terrain—maybe that's how you feel about your spiritual identity—you are just discovering who you are.

Chapter 11

Divine Energy Acceleration – Vibration

THE LAST TIME I REMEMBER MEDITATING WAS about twelve years ago. Very sadly, that's the last time I can remember doing something to center, rejuvenate, and connect myself to Divine consciousness. Of course back then we didn't call it Divine consciousness or at least I don't remember that the term was widely used. Anyway, I was writing this chapter and walked into a healing store to browse around a bit; I'm always gathering data on energy and vibration of the Divine kind. So here I am looking around and my eye kept going back over the meditation CD by Kelly Howell. So I'm reading the back jacket to the CD and she starts out by saying, *"maybe you've tried to meditate before but lost interest"* and I naturally think, *"Hey, anything to jump start me and get me back on track with rejuvenating myself, I'm on board."* Besides, it had been years since I had sat in front of the CD player with

Betty Bethards guided meditation and techniques. If I were going to dig those jewels out in order to brush up on re-reading her books and listening to her cassette tapes, I might spend some time reacquainting myself. Cassette tapes should clue you into how old my meditation stuff is.

Yep, and here Kelly Howell was giving me an alternative method of learning to quiet the mind and enter into deep meditation that sometimes takes years of practice. Her meditation was a fancy, clinically proven brain wave therapy used and studied by biofeedback therapists and she was claiming her CD could open the door to the theta state of advanced meditation. She gave a 30-minute and a 60-minute version. So naturally I was intrigued, and I bought the CD.

Woweee, I nearly knocked my own socks off! What an experience. My ears were ringing, and I felt this rush of vibration pulsing through me and I finished up the meditation session with my palms tingling. I hadn't had quite this experience before—it's amazing what new technology can do for you. Oh, and this was before I incorporated crystal vibration into the session.

You have to understand that I've worked with healing touch, massage, and meditation years ago, and I hadn't had this kind of energy manifestation until after I had activated my light-body. This depth of Divine vibrational energy resonance was previously not experienced by me.

My funny story is this—I went to sit on the edge of my bed to plug back in the boom-box that I had taken to my writing room for the meditation. Before I got the plug close to the outlet my bedside table lamp lit up. This is a touch lamp, meaning you have to physically touch it to make it go on. Well my lightbody energy being reactivated by the meditation I'm certain, sure was touching everything in its path.

Not only did my lamp light up which made me smile, but my computer screen when I turned on my computer, turned a magenta color. The color magenta has a special significance as I learned when next I went on-line to research Vibrational Energy Medicine.

My husband had to unplug the computer monitor for me and plug it back in to reset the screen—so I wouldn't have to do the rest of my research or read email on a magenta screen. This is a wow for me to have this kind of stuff manifesting after only the first meditation session. I could hardly wait for the next morning meditation to see what Divine Father revealed to me next time.

The other person who has entered my life is, Lisa Keyes, whom I mentioned in the Chapter 7, and her phenomenal teachings of the sacred anointing ceremony, which has shifted my vibration into what I like to call "overdrive" with her enlightening process, which opens portals to divine consciousness for us. She has spent years in divine service to us so she could bring us the wisdom she gathered along the way. She started out as an ordained minister in charismatic Christianity and then over time becoming more "outside the box" and outgrew that to begin questioning more of what we weren't being told. Lisa went on this huge journey and quest to learn more about God, about Jesus, Creator of this universe, and the Divine (whatever name deems more comfortable for the individual reading this).

She explains that, *in seeking the truth it lead her to the very ancient reading called the Dead Sea Scrolls, Gnostic Christianity, the Apocrypha, the unknown saints of St. Thomas, Mother Mary, the first two thousand years of Christianity and religion, and as she read these books and started digging more thoroughly as well as doing studies with Gnostic Christianity, she realized why for centuries the church had shut these books out. Because they were way more empowering than all the other books she had previously read and she found out that we were truly the divine spark, and that we are created in the image of God and that we are way more empowered than she had ever dreamed of.*

As she was reading about our true divine nature, she came across the ancient ceremony that the Mystics would do, and as she started doing the ancient anointing process over her life the things she wanted and needed for breakthrough began to happen. This is when she started to learn who her higher self was—she was making a connection with this truer divine presence which is herself. She has been sharing this process with her clients and they have encouraged her to get the message out to us about our divinity.

My husband and I can testify that the process is wonderfully effective and divinely empowering—many thanks and gratitude to Lisa for her courage and wisdom. This is testimony as well to the ascension that we are awakening to our divine vibration by tapping into our divine spiritual DNA.

Anne Christine Tooley is the author of the *Vibrational Energy Medicine* web site and she talks about DNA this way: The Kabbalah Tree of Life is the blueprint of ALL life. DNA maps to the Kabbalah Tree of Life, so it is possible for our DNA to…eventually obtain spiritual enlightenment.

She goes on to explain that scientists are now discovering that DNA actually emits *light*, and that Russian scientist, Pjotr Garjajev, was able to intercept communication from a DNA molecule in the form of ultraviolet photons, which again is *light*! Furthermore, she has researched how DNA is accessed via color, light, sound, crystals and stones, sacred geometry and other holistic modalities.

So you can see the correlation between these scientific datum and the soft laser therapy I spoke of earlier, which transmits healing light and color to the cellular level of living organisms and most importantly people and animals. Why wouldn't this work? After all we have been discussing how our energy frequency or vibration is given to us by our Divine Father in the form of spiritual DNA. Just like we are the electrical light source for our bodies, our electrical light source for our DNA comes from spirit. It doesn't take a rocket scientist though to figure out that once you leave your body that there is nobody home. You've taken your light with you. That's how the doctors can pronounce you dead. Get it! You're no longer there. As long as you're in your body they can't pronounce you dead because the lights are still on—well, no kidding.

Our spiritual light is the energy that keeps all their machines and gadgets flashing and registering activity.

No brain-wave activity means you're out of the body and watching from a distance while the medical team tries to revive you, or you are already on your way to the beautiful spiritual realm of Divine home. And unless you're going to be a near-death experience candidate you aren't coming back into that hunk of meat lying lifeless on the hospital bed.

As discussed in Richard Gerber's book, Vibrational Medicine, there are two fundamentally different kinds of energy, which according to William

Tiller, a Stanford physicist, is evident in the Tiller-Einstein model. The first kind of energy is *Electromagnetic energy*, which functions in a positive space/time universe and is bound by the laws limiting the speed of light; and the second kind of energy is *Magnetoelectric energy*, or the *"life force energy"* which works in a negative space/time where faster than light movement is possible.

The kind of energy involved in vibrational medicine is this second energy. The energy fields that surround the physical body are called the *"subtle energy bodies"* and are composed of energy that is not visible or felt by the five physical senses.

For a quick look at these subtle energy bodies you have, which resemble layers of an onion, starting closest to your physical body is the etheric body, next to that is astral or emotional body, then the mental body and on the very outside of all the bodies you have the spiritual or casual body. From those energy bodies closest to you to the outermost energy body, you have different rates of vibration, which makes the highest vibrational level being your spiritual body.

The rate of your vibration is *THE vital key* to your earth life existence. Because the higher your vibration rate the more you are reaching your spiritual vibration potential and the healthier you are to be around.

I can explain this better in the Vibratory Scale below. This information is taken from the book, *Power vs. Force*, by David Hawkins, M.D., Ph.D. This model outlines how individual qualities of mind rank in terms of vibration, on a scale of 20 to 600.

QUALITY	LOG	EMOTION
Peace	600	Bliss
Joy	540	Serenity
Love	500	Reverence
Reason	400	Understanding
Acceptance	350	Forgiveness
Willingness	310	Optimism
Neutrality	250	Trust
Courage	200	Affirmation
Pride	175	Scorn
Anger	150	Hate
Desire	125	Craving
Fear	100	Anxiety
Grief	75	Regret

Apathy	50	Despair
Guilt	30	Blame
Shame	20	Humiliation

FIG. 1: SCALE OF CONSCIOUSNESS

Dr. Hawkins has researched how the vibration rates affect us and it is nicely explained for us in Colin Tipping's book, *Radical Manifestation,* where Tipping explains how low-vibration people tend to *"regularly experience emotions like anger, fear, resentment, jealousy, cynicism, apathy and other negative emotions. They tend to have a preponderance of core-negative beliefs. They tend to be energy vampires, taking more out of the system than they put in. They tend to lay blame and justify."* Wow, can't you just think of a few individuals that fit this category? Then there's the high-vibration folks who, Tipping goes on to explain, *"are people who are likely to be free of most negative emotions and will have a predominance of core-positive beliefs. These people are likely to be bright, happy, open-minded, likable, clear, cooperative and creative. High-vibration people are more apt to experience emotions like appreciation, gratitude, compassion, humility and love than those of a more negative nature. They are more likely to draw on the finer energy coming from Spirit and eschew energy that emanates from Ego. People of high vibration usually have high integrity…and put a lot more into a system than they take out, as well as, give energy to those around them rather than seek to draw it from others.*

Tipping wraps up by saying, it feels good to be in their presence.

So now that you start to see the bigger picture here of what shape you're in energy-wise, you are probably starting to notice some things about yourself or others that need a little energy adjustment. So where does one go to get an adjustment of energy? Lucky for those with computers and internet, there are quite a few avenues you can look into. I would say, though, that often the easiest ones are the simplest ones and depending upon how elaborate you want to get, the energy healing modalities can range in cost, as well.

Maybe right about here, you're wondering what any of this has to do with living your life in an earth suit. Let's look at this a little more closely. Say you are around someone who drains you. Say you start to feel as awful as they do; maybe you find yourself spiralling down the vibration scale somewhere around the vibration of Anger/Hate rate 150.

How do you feel at this point? Do you think you're able to see things in a forgiving light and with love and grace? Not a chance. So what has just happened to you?

Well, aside from the usual list of things that you can think of that you are probably feeling—stressed, upset, too tired to do anything but flop into bed, and maybe even spiraling down on the scale even further to guilt/blame rate 30—you are not in any state to be making decisions.

Nor are you going to be able to function at a level that is therapeutic to be around. In other words you're a mess. You can't be expected to fight your way out of a paper bag. It goes without saying, you are no joy to be around. In fact, you could do us all a favor and just take a time-out, go someplace comforting and gather yourself together. This low-vibration is your Ego playing havoc with you. Ego is slamming your around and metaphorically tromping on you.

How do you combat Ego? You sic Spiritual energy on Ego.

One thing I've learned is that low-energy vibration and high-energy vibration cannot exist together. So you are in either high or low, but never both at the same time. It's like a light bulb—it can't be both on and off at the same time.

How do you, then, get yourself out of the mess you're in?

Simply raise your energy.

It's not rocket science. It is simply energy science.

And if you aren't an energy-healing expert, then find yourself one. Someone who can heal your energy upset. Even better, find a natural energy healer who can show you how to maintain your high-vibration or quickly repair a low-vibration. The fast fixes like high energy drinks or caffeine drinks are a false fix, they don't care if you stay feeling good or not, in fact they get your repeat business if you start to feel drained and stressed and life-less.

Now just because I've just said that about caffeine and such, does not mean I'm going to give up my one cup of coffee with French vanilla creamer in the morning.

But now when I need, metaphorically speaking, something to raise my energy, I'm not going to be relying on coffee. Doesn't it make sense that if we are light-energy-vibration spirit beings that we get our energy from an energy support system?

So I ask you, what have you learned thus far?

Well, you've heard me rant on about how we are spiritual light bodies. That our creator is Divine Father. Isn't it also, Divine Father, who created the universe and the earth with all its Divine cosmic elements?

I'm hoping by now you know the answer to this.

But if you don't then here's the deal, you now get to look at energy creation beyond yourself.

In chemistry class I learned about the electrical charge of electrons, protons, and neutrons and how each of the molecules in the Element Scale has a weight and electrical charge value. Think about it. Everything is made up of molecules of energy. Our light bodies or spiritual bodies are a thriving vortex of energy which encompasses us from our spiritual and physical bodies, clear down to the depth of our cells and then even more minute into the power house of each cell, the Golgi body and Mitochondria. These molecules are performing functions unseen to the naked eye right under our very noses every single day of our lives.

Divine Father knew what He was doing when He designed us in His image. He wasn't just goofing around or half asleep when He designed us, and the universe. He put His whole heart into manifesting us to be these perfect energy bodies, with a heart to circulate the blood and oxygen to our cells to keep the physical body functioning at its best. We are a perfect work of art and energy. So is our earth and the plants and animals a perfect work of art and energy. Have you ever stopped to think about why the earth?

Why would it be made perfectly to support life, the plants giving off oxygen, which supports physical life? We weren't an experiment.

We weren't some random Big Bang theory that somebody threw together on the spur of the moment and hoped the whole thing would work out.

Nope, Divine Father has created us in a perfect plan of existence. The food we eat was created for us, vegetables and meat and fish, all Divine Father creation. The earth for us to dwell upon while we are in our bodies was again, all Divine Father creation. The water we drink, which our physical bodies are made up of 70% water, again all Divine Father creation. None of this is random accident. This whole support system of interrelated and interdependent life systems are here for a specific function and all of it is driven by energy.

All life is interlinked—trees are alive to give us oxygen and process carbon dioxide which we breathe out—earth is alive and fashioning water and harvest and gravity for us, so we can drink water, eat harvest, and not float off into the atmosphere—earth is the very support system divinely created for us. So if you feel you aren't loved by Divine Father, think again about all the work and thought and perfection He went to the trouble to create for us all the way back to first creation and when we were just a twinkle in His eye.

Back to the energy discussion—the earth is here, just like the plants and other facets of life are here to support us.

Divine Father has gone to a whole lot of trouble to make sure we are supported in this universe. So where can our subtle energy bodies and our physical body get plugged in to recharge, if not with energy drinks and coffee?

This is where we look at turning our thoughts to earth. Earth is our support system— regardless of how bad we treat earth—it is still here for us and trying to hang in there for us no matter how we are trying to destroy her with pollution and nuclear waste and all the other things you can think of that we do to earth.

Earth is designed to give up her body for our needs and support.

Earth also has a spirit energy given to her by Divine Father. I will demonstrate how this works for us in a moment.

We all have taken a science class in school, but for simplification and to refresh our memory—we all know Energy can have either positive or negative effects. Positive and negative energy can cancel each other out. These are just some of the elemental laws of physics, science, etc. What we may not have learned in science classroom is that the same vibration we have and each of our organs have and different microorganisms have—there's a specific vibration rate for each. I mentioned how earth is designed to support us and you can see how that works, well now let's take a look at something less commonly understood by the general public.

That earth gives up her bits and parts like in crystals and rocks and each of these have their vibratory rate as well. What I didn't know until I started reading Lynn McTaggart's book, *Intention Experiment*, was that science has proved that plants have an intelligence that is designed to complement our own. Meaning plants can feel what we are thinking. Yes, they react to us. If we are thinking just a thought about burning a leaf on a plant it starts to freak out and we can measure with scientific machines the plant's reactions to us. Plants have a frequency-vibration-resonance, if you will. The common Cold microorganism has a frequency of 58 megahertz or Mhz. The Flu microorganism has a frequency of 42 Mhz. Death causing Cancer has a frequency of 42 Mhz. And our bodily death process begins at 25 Mhz. That is to say—in a manner of speaking—when we are getting a cold or flu we are leaking our energy out to the point these microorganisms can then take over and start wrecking their havoc on us.

You are probably starting to see the trend of what the lower-vibrations mean to us in terms of our physical health. I'm giving you these trends to help you start thinking about your own rate of vibration and what you can do to raise your energy vibration or get plugged in to earth to get back your highest vibration rate.

You also saw in my earlier example above how peace, joy, and love are at the highest vibration rate of 600, 540, and 500.

A great crystal researcher, Kaitlyn Keyt, at *VibesUp.com*, has done some wonderful discoveries in the area of raising your energy. I happen to be sitting on a crystal mat infused with Rose oil (320 Mhz) vibration while I write this chapter and at this point my vibration is such that mental clarity and high energy needed to bring clear thought is working for me very nicely. I'm having no writing blocks. In fact, I can hardly get the words down on paper fast enough for the flow at which they are coming to me. Wouldn't it be nice to feel this way at work? Around other people? In our love relationships? With our children? At school?

Wouldn't it be divine for our children to have enough energy to ward off hyperactivity caused by their sensitivity to their environment? Wouldn't it be nice to have energy enough to enjoy life and still have enough to share with others and bring their energy up? This is how we can love each other and be operating at our very best energy level—by tapping into our earth recharge element—and it is given to us freely and most generously by earth herself. You've heard the saying, *"we need to protect our earth."* Well this is why. Because she is literally keeping our physical bodies fed, watered and electrically nurtured. Without her our physical bodies would drop in energy to 25 Mhz or less—our physical body would be dying or dead.

Let's look at some other vibration rates. Kaitlyn has researched and found out our brain frequency-vibration-resonance is at 72-90 Mhz. Just think how much clearer we could think and how much more we could remember if we are supplying just the right amount of natural energy to the brain.

The body, when at optimum vibration is between 62-68 Mhz. Remember I talked about how the rates of disease are down around the 58 Mhz level or less. Well there's not much of a range between disease at 58 Mhz and body vibration 62-68 Mhz.

To me, this means that we are pretty susceptible to disease if we fluctuate even 10 degrees. This ought to get your attention, right? You are probably starting to see how raising your energy can be healthful. Keeping ourselves mentally, physically, and emotionally healthy is very vital to us. Keeping your Spiritual energy field fed is another whole realm of which we need to be conscious about and nurture as well.

Okay, here's some other energy values you may like to know. According to Kaitlyn our Processed food vibrates at zero (0 Mhz.). Meaning you get no energy fed to you by processed food. Wild, huh? Fresh produce feeds your energy vibration with up to 15 Mhz. Better than processed food, right! Dry herbs vibrate at 12-22 Mhz. Fresh herbs at 20-27 Mhz. Now get this—essential oil vibrations are between 52-320 Mhz. Are you starting to see something going on here? I saved the best for last—Rose oil in its best form is at the highest vibration in nature at 320 Mhz. Think about it—as far back as the language of flowers began, Roses were a flower to give to represent our love to the person we are gifting them too. This was established back before they had machines to measure vibration rate. Rose oil has a high vibration of 320 Mhz, and if you look at the vibration scale for love you find love's vibration is 500Mhz and Divine Father is love in the purest form. Aren't you starting to see that the higher our vibration the closer we are to our natural spiritual resonance and the closer to being able to dwell in the God consciousness realm? It's like Divine Father knew we were going to need help and He has supplied us the tools to find our way back to Him and our best divine state of being. Sounds good to me, anyway.

Okay, so what does this mean to you and me?

It means that we can raise our energy vibration with things supplied by earth. I'm talking things from nature are literally nurturing, feeding and supporting us throughout the day.

Did you know our feet have 50,000 receptors on the bottom of them? Think about it. We were happiest as children running around bare foot in the dirt and grass and whatever else we could get into.

Earth literally feeds us what we need this way. And guess what? Crystals, minerals, rocks have a vibration that feed us energy through our feet if we are walking barefoot directly on the earth. Not on concrete or asphalt or rubber soles which act to break the contact with earth. I'm talking about walking directly ON the earth.

Get this—just like plants, crystals have also been proven to be able to read us so well that they have the ability to turn on what energy element we need from them, and when we have had enough energy fed to us they turn off the energy. You get what you need and no more!

Remember as a kid most of us had this seemingly unlimited energy supply. Remember, we were told to go outside and play? Well we were getting dirty and playing with and on the earth, climbing trees, getting sunshine, getting plugged into our energy source.

Here's a sobering fact amidst all this. Synthetics are man-made. They are not Divine Father made to really support physical life. Synthetic *"anything"* can bring an energy, but they are not designed to read us and know how much energy to bring us or when to back off the energy. We wear synthetic fiber clothing, brush our hair with synthetic bristle brushes, take synthetic-made drugs, walk upon synthetic made surfaces. Rubber soled shoes are synthetic and rubber blocks the conductivity of energy. Synthetic made medications cannot know how much the body needs, they just dose us with whatever level they are set to dose us. There is no Divine nature intelligence at work here. In contrast, now let's take aspirin for instance. Its elements come from nature and the cardiac doctors (heart and circulatory doctors alike) prescribe this a lot to maintain heart health in adults. You've probably seen the commercials on TV about aspirin.

You're also being bombarded on the TV by the pharmaceutical industry who makes all the synthetic drugs for this and that, which carry some scary side effects and they may be contributing no energy value to you at all.

I'm not saying that we can eliminate all synthetics from our lives, but we can search out the things that raise our energy to a healthy vibration. In nature we are co-existing with our combined plant, animal, crystal, flower, human intelligence given to us by Divine Father.

Crystals ground up in the earth's crust from years of earth movement and activity have an intelligence that comes with knowing how much human bodies need and when to back off. They each supply us with energy—some are specific to block negativity, boost mental clarity, open us to heart Chakra love, and basically support any number of physical and spiritual energy needs. Imagine this new world of discovery for yourself—what you could learn.

Crystal energy supply is not something I learned in any of my chemistry classes, microbiology classes, biology classes, or any other classes taught at the traditional schools I attended. Until now. The Holistic Health realm is available through our colleges now, thank goodness. This is the day and age where you learn beyond what your parents were taught in school and passed on to you. I have included an Appendix A, in the back of this book, to give you an idea of the instruments that are available to man to measure this type of energy vibration.

Let's take this one step further and look at the energy our thoughts and intentions have. Did you know that you can change energy levels of people around you? According to Dr. Hawkins, if you are vibrating energy at a level of around 350, which is up there around the acceptance/forgiveness level, then you can be counteracting 200,000 people below the level of 200. Hawkins goes on to point out, that if you are vibrating at the energy level of 500, which is up there with love/reverence level, then you can be counteracting 750,000 people below 200. So here's something to consider—if you are one of those worried about losing your job, which is down around the vibration of 100 where fear hangs out, then you would do well to hang out with others at work who are vibrating with high energy. If you can't find anyone at work healthy enough to hang out with, then get your energy vibration raised by other means.

If you can spend just a little bit of time studying the Scale of Consciousness I bet it wouldn't take you long to be able to just look at someone on the street and gauge where their vibration is at. Pride (someone being boastful) is pretty easy to spot. Anger, fear, and grief are also pretty easy to spot. When someone is displaying courage or a willingness to listen to or do something then you are looking at someone who is better off—they are nearer the top end of the higher vibrations.

Well peace, joy, and love speak for themselves—and we may not even know at first that the person is vibrating this high except when we are feeling them affect us in a good vibe way. Of course, when a person smiles a genuine smile, this pretty much clues us in and we find ourselves smiling back.

The countenance of Jesus as depicted by actors in the Bible movies, is a countenance of peace and higher.

No matter what is being thrown His way he is at peace. If you guessed that His vibration is up there at 600 or higher, you are close. Actually, closer to 1,000 Mhz, according to Dr. Hawkins.

Look at the Dali Lama's face. Wouldn't you also say his vibration has to be up there with peace vibration? This is something to try to attain for oneself, wouldn't you think? It is now possible with the technology we have. You just need to want it for yourself and find your energy vibration healer.

You're starting to see where I'm going here, right? We are capable of affecting each other with our light-body energy level. All we need to do to feel better and be healthy is to bring our energy up. Bottom line, since we are pure divine energy source then what we feel and think can have a big impact upon our lives both physically as Ego and spiritually as Divine light bodies. If you need to feel lighter and brighter than it is as simple as raising your energy level!

Chapter 12

New Age Vibration and Indigo Children

THE DNA CHANGES THAT HUMAN-KIND HAS UNDERGONE has been emerging under our very noses and most of the changes taking place have been in children. It is believed that this new age vibration is no coincidence. Remember, I talked about there being no coincidences—just divine timing. This chapter is more about Divine timing. More about Divine Spiritual DNA.

The phenomenon has been observed in China since around the 1970's. According to research by Drunvalo Melchizedek and noted in volume two, *"The Ancient Secret of the Flower of Life, in the chapter on The New Children*, there was a newly mutated child, who became noticed by the world—who could *"see"* with his ears. Yes, you heard me correctly. It gets even better. This new race of children started cropping up all over the place and by the 1980's, in the United States, scientists dubbed them with the name, *"Indigo Children."*

Melchizedek goes on to explain, that the new age vibration children now make up 80-90% of the children born in the U.S.; this is according to scientific research which was compiled by author's, Jan Tober and Lee Carroll. The research includes accounts from doctors, psychologists, and scientists who have taken their findings seriously enough to conduct scientifically controlled experiments to measure the validity of what they were seeing. What I think is worth mentioning here, beyond all the scientific data, is that these spiritual children are here for you and I to learn from. They are here to teach us. That's if we can get out of our own way and wake up to smell the roses. I don't know about you but I love the way roses smell—both literally and spiritually.

What the scientists were discovering was astounding. Astounding if you are not yet convinced we are all Divine spiritual beings. Astounding, I believe, if you haven't yet received enough testimony from traditional venues to *"God created us in His image."* To me, it has always been pretty clear that *"With God all things are possible."* I have always known this to be true.

Like I mentioned early on about being a frustrated child and not being able to levitate or materialize things; it didn't change my gut nagging at me that there was more to this life than meets the eye.

Beginning at childhood, I've transformed into a fully aware adult and like I have discovered, there are tools out in the world for self-discovery. It has become my story about the transmutation of energy. Which, I've already gone into in the last chapter and will expand upon for you here.

This chapter just expands upon and gives case study to the facts that aren't wanting to be ignored with the coming of this new vibration age. We are being shocked awake, so to speak. Of course, as Ego's having our merry way, we can deny our way out of just about anything—deny it exists, deny we've seen it, deny we've heard about it, deny that it is possible—after God has proclaimed for all to witness that with Him all things are possible. Again, I must reiterate, that you are where you are at spiritually, so if you aren't ready to hear more than what you already know, it is just where you are at spiritually. I repeat—it doesn't make you wrong or right—it just makes you where you are at in your level of spiritual knowledge.

Hey, if you aren't able to raise your energy high enough to reach willingness/optimism at 310 on the vibration scale, then your vibration isn't going to be conducive to learning new knowledge anyway. Also, remember, I think that it is okay for you to be where you are at with your state of knowledge—we are all on our own timing with Divine Father revelations. We all get to the same place eventually—once we drop our earth suits it's good-bye to the old ego knowledge and hello divine light knowledge. So if you don't get it this time around, not to worry, you'll work your way there some other day.

That being said, Indigo Children and Adults are brilliant—yes, there are adults who are extraordinary in their manifestation on this earth, as well. Melchizedek's further research found this: that the Indigos have an IQ that averages around 130, with that being the lower end of the range—while the norm for this vibrational child is up in the genius range of 160 or higher. The significance is; that while an IQ of 130 is not considered "genius", you have to understand that an IQ of 130 used to only be one in 10,000 persons. The norm now has shifted.

What you might not know about this brilliant new vibrational child is that our education system is not equipped to figure them out; most teachers have judged this new human race as problematic or defective. Who comes to your mind? Yes. The ADD and ADHD diagnosed child or person.

The problem, you see, is with the educational system and not knowing how to manage these brilliant and gifted children.

Frankly speaking, these children are bored with us. Their energy vibration is off the scale and so we try to drug them back into submission. If we just balanced their energy vibration instead of drugging them, they would thrive and we would not be freaking out over how to handle that much energy pouring through.

Simply speaking—the trick here is balancing energy vibration. It's like having the sound on the radio turned up and the noise becomes so grating on your nerves that you quickly reach for the volume button to turn it down or shut it up. Balance is key. Harmonics is key. Vibration is key.

How do you then balance this kind of energy? Go back to the chapter before and pay closer attention if you don't readily come up with the answer.

Simply use the energy tools—crystals of the earth.

Oh yeah, I haven't mentioned that Indigo children (or adults) could use some harmonizing energy. Well, the perfect divine answer is always available to us. For example, Quartz, is an amplifier of energy vibration. They used this in the old "Quartz" radios before TV was invented. Guess what—our computers are made up of carbon, just like our bodies are carbon molecules (with some other stuff, of course) and carbon is in the earth and when heated and compressed it forms Diamonds. Viola—a quick biology and chemistry tidbit for you. Quartz carries its own intelligence vibration—carbon carries its own intelligence vibration and no wonder we think our computers are amazing works of art. That is when they aren't acting up and being finicky.

Remember I mentioned earlier that my computer monitor screen went a magenta color when I sat down and turned it on after I had blown my socks off meditating? Well, golly gee, the computer monitor was reading me. Not far-fetched. Just vibrational science. Remember I mentioned that my table lamp went on without me touching it—well, golly gee, my vibration turned it on. I didn't even have to touch it with my physical finger.

See how this energy is all around us, built into us as Spiritual DNA. Are you starting to see how changing your vibration can change your quality of life?

Both in the body and out of it—we are affecting each other and the environment around us. The trick is to be kind with it—to yourself and others.

A hug carries so many facets of love vibration, comfort, and caring—you see why God gave us arms instead of feelers, antennas, or furry legs.

Our pets feed us warm fuzzy energy when we hug them. We are all on this earth to support and take care *with* each other. We are here to *learn how* to take care with each other. This is part of the spiritual college we signed up for on the other side. And here you thought it was all about who gets the last word in and who comes out on top. Hmmm, that would be Ego playing havoc again.

Back to the topic at hand—Indigos. In Drunvalo Melchizedek's volume two, he goes on to tell us all the facts from the scientific validation point of research. According to his fact findings—these children are able to demonstrate that whatever they think becomes reality. In essence, what you think is what you get. The Chinese government got involved with the research and found that these gifted children are able to demonstrate abilities that are truly difficult to accept inside our "normal" reality.

For instance, in 1985 *Omni Magazine* was present in China to observe the phenomenon and found that it was true—that the Chinese government claimed that these children, when blindfolded, could "see" either with their ears, nose, mouth, tongue, armpits, hands or feet. Each child was different and their vision from these unheard of areas was perfect, meaning these tests were not just a percentage right some of the time—the tests were flawless.

Drunvalo goes on to explain, that *Omni* conducted their own examination of these children in a way that ruled out any possible cheating—they were leaving nothing to chance. So they selected and took a stack of books and at random selected one of them, then opened the book at random and ripped out a page and crumpled it into a small ball. *Omni* then placed it in the armpit of one of these children—and the child could read every word on the page perfectly! After many varied tests—*Omni* became convinced as had the Chinese government, that the phenomenon was real—even if they could not explain how these kids were doing it. The report by *Omni* was released in their January 1985 issue.

So you are seeing a tip of the iceberg with this—it has started—our new and improved link to our spiritual heritage and the energy vibration phenomenon that we are all capable of developing. You heard me right—God gave us all the same spiritual DNA—what we do with it is up to our free will choice.

And it's no wonder He has sent in back-ups to revive us of the faith Jesus tried to evoke in us way back when He was here walking among us. Divine Father is all around us—He's in us as spiritual DNA energy—He hasn't forsaken us no matter what we might think to the contrary.

Divine Father is always on top of our growth and development—while not interfering with our free will to learn what we have come here to learn. We are given free will by His choice. What we do with our freedom to muck it up or make it better is up to us. Maybe you are starting to see this—Yes? Just maybe you are starting to see outside the box we have built around ourselves—funny human bodies that we are.

What we are discovering as the energy shifts and the energy of awakening is enlightening us to develop our spiritual vibration, is that concepts that used to sound far-fetched are becoming scientifically verifiable, and easily measured. Lynne McTaggart has gone to great lengths to bring together unexplained phenomenon with scientific data to the public for our perusal. Then there is the unexplained phenomenon of spontaneity or something called synchronicity, which is tied directly to elevated spiritual vibration. This is where we are tapping into our higher Divine self, usually with the aide of someone who is a facilitator or encouragement in the form of seeking divine answers. This latter realm is being witnessed by more and more spiritually inclined individuals, where the truth is being sought out and is finally available in a language we can at least comprehend.

I was watching a talk show host one morning, and she was bringing a child prodigy story to the world that day. I remember there were three guests on the show that morning—Colton Burpo, Dr. Mary C. Neal, and Akiane Kramarik. Both Colton and Mary were there to talk about their near death experiences. I later went out and bought their books. But it was Akiane, who painted the picture she named, *Prince of Peace*, which is clearly the flawless painting of Jesus—the thing so amazing was this child was only eight when she painted this likeness of Jesus. Even more revealing was what Colton Burpo said when he saw the painting. Colton declared, *"That one's right."*

Clearly he is remembering his near death experience where he visited heaven and spent some time with God, Jesus, the angels, and yes, the animals.

Colton was able to confirm that the painting by Akiane was the same Jesus he saw in heaven.

Colton came back with a message for us from Jesus, too. I won't ruin the story for you by giving away the facets of it, but if you care to read Colton's story you can find his book on the internet.

Do you begin to wonder why these Indigo Children like Akiane and the others have incarnated at this particular time? You think they might have something to teach us? Is it any wonder your child is trying to get your attention—or our attention? If we learn how to raise these gifted new spirits of high vibration then we will be doing all of mankind a favor—for they have incarnated for us.

Half of the fun is looking into this for yourself—with your ego left at the door so you'll not be missing the messages. For more on Akiane's painting, you can go to artakiane.com.

Besides the higher vibration rate of the Indigo children and adults, there are other people who have contributions to the validation of energy vibration importance. To attest to how our energy frequency can physically affect other objects and people around you, there is Dr. William Braud and his colleagues at the Mind Science Foundation in San Antonio. They conducted an experiment in a lab dish, which proved that people, with their thoughts and energy, could slow down the rate that red blood cells die. Phenomenal to say the least! This was a *"bio-PK"* experiment, which means this experiment focused around the study of how psychokinesis affects other biological organisms. Remember, in an earlier chapter where I talked about the plant that freaked out (all this registered on the polygraph) when someone approached the plant with the thought of burning a leaf on the plant. This was an experiment, by the way, by Cleve Backster. Here's another example of how we affect energy with our thought vibration.

This one is a research study by Dr. Masaru Emoto, where he wrote on a piece of paper a higher vibrational word like *"love"* or *"joy"* and taped the piece of paper onto the glass of water. Then he froze the water and looked at the resulting water crystals under a microscope—the beautiful water crystal patterns were pure in color and had perfect symmetry.

Then he did the same experiment with a piece of paper that had lower vibrational words like *"hate"* or *"anger"* taped onto the glass, and those water crystals when frozen were rough, opaque, and in a state of chaos.

Are you starting to see how energy plays an enormous role in our lives? How we can be conductors and projectors of either good or bad energy—how this can be felt by every living organism on this planet?

Don't you think if this is all going on behind the physical scene that it wouldn't also being going on within the spiritual body realm?

Again, just because we can't see it with the human eye, doesn't mean it is not playing a huge role in our existence. Our Spiritual DNA is the powerhouse where all this energy is being stored and released without much thought, apparently, going into it.

Here's my most current account of an encounter with a fellow student. Recently, I started to attend college again. After the nursing program I didn't think I'd ever be able to confront taking classes again, but I guess it's kind of like giving birth. You tell yourself, never again, and then you forget how painful the process and you blissfully do it again.

Well in my Crystal class, I sat next to a young woman who was an Astro-physicist. We introduced ourselves to the class and then midway through lecture the student I sat next to, turned to me and in a fascinated voice, suddenly tells me that she could *"see"* my aura. She had my full attention. At this point neither of us were paying attention to the instructor who was in the middle of lecture. What my classmate said to me was my aura was bright white and then she tried to describe it with her hands as radiating up and around me and had this twinkling quality. Trying to help her with the description, I asked her if she meant that I sparkled and she happily exclaimed, "Yes!"

We were in our own little world of sharing our thoughts on how I thought she was an intuitive seer. I don't see auras to my knowledge, but I was able to tell her I am a *"feeler"* meaning I feel or know things.

So we got into this whispered exchange of how we each have our unique way of using our senses to perceive things. I thought this was an exhilarating way to start out the day in class. What I also told the young woman I sat next to was that I don't know if it had anything to do with her *"seeing"* my aura, but I happened to be sitting on my crystal mat.

Not only was I sitting on my crystal mat, but I was wearing a crystal pendant, had crystal bracelets on both wrists, was drinking water from a bottle infused with crystals, oh and let's not forget the insoles of my shoes where cut-outs from a crystal mat like the one I was sitting upon. You think that had anything to do with the aura she was *"seeing?"*

I thought it was perfect validation to how crystal energy supports us. From this unexpected encounter, I learned that my intuition about raising my vibration with crystals was right on target.

My point is this, I didn't have to do anything special to have my energy vibration crystals working for me. I just had to be wearing them! They do the rest!

Now, wouldn't it be much better to have learned this as a child, so I could have had better mental clarity, memory, and energy for my school studies? Talk about things being right under our very noses.

There are plenty of folks awakening to these new frequencies and what they mean for all of us. Don't you think it's time we start paying attention to who we are as spiritual energy vibration—and what we can do to make some positive changes for all our benefit?

How about—Raise Your Vibration and Change Your life!

Now here is *the* pivotal question: If plants can read our thoughts and animals can read us, and crystals can read us and supply us with supporting energy frequencies—what are we humans capable of?

Don't forget we are created in His image. I've been trying to help connect you to your heritage all the way through this book. You have seen above just a few examples of—*All Things Are Possible with Divine Father.*

Don't you see how beautifully designed you are—how beautifully spiritual! You are a beautiful vibration of Divine Light! Say hello to your true self!

Chapter 13

Gear Up for the Ascension with these Exercises

MELCHIZEDEK TALKS ABOUT THE REASONS FOR DEVEL-
OPING ourselves for the fourth dimension—our transition—the great historical event surrounding our ascension. Gregg Braden and James Twyman and the *Book of Revelations*, to name a few, all elude to this spiritual event. Some believe it is happening now, some give actual dates of this event and when it will start—the point is whether it is happening now or eventually will, it is my belief that we are ahead of the game if we at least recognize we are vibrational spirit beings. My focus is not going to be taken off track from you, by pending earth circumstances.

Spirit heaven is home anyway—not this place. This is just a place we come to play around with lessons. Betty Bethards will tell you this. Melchizedek will tell you this. All great spiritually-connected souls will tell you this. So let's work on developing us—develop our divine spirit minds and bodies.

How does one develop themselves? By seeking your truth…and by being responsible.

Sounds simple and yet complex all at the same time. It's like this—when you decide to be responsible the whole universe divinely shifts. You can't develop or grow or flourish or transcend by sticking your head in the ground. You must come out of hiding. Actively seek truths. This action alone will start you on the path to being responsible.

It doesn't matter what you have believed to be a truth up to now—you can decide to expand upon what you think you know at any time of day or night or any year.

Raising your energy vibration can greatly assist you! It can actually mean the difference between succeeding or floundering. Think about how high your energy needs to be to arrive at Willingness. Willingness is where you are optimistic about life! So if you are feeling anything less than willing and optimistic, it's time to connect yourself to crystal energy

Quartz is a great facilitator in raising energy vibration, it's an easy place to start. I've given you some references to websites to also get you started. If you want to go all out, then you can seek out a Reiki energy healer, a meditation facilitator, and the list goes on.

You have a choice. Free will choice. This is built into you.

By Divine Father.

So you can take as long or as fast as you want to accomplish your growth. Divine Father is behind you whether you decide to do something now or next year or (next lifetime if you can imagine that for yourself).

Just because you might not yet be able to perceive or conceive of the idea or concept of spiritual transition it doesn't mean you are not going to be faced with the process. This is the transformation each of us makes from physical world to spiritual world. It will happen to each of us as our earth suit dies off. Just like it can happen in a natural disaster, a huge number of the human population has already discovered the spirit world in an abrupt fashion.

Part of the Ascension process is shifting energy vibration. You may remember we gave a definition of ascension back in chapter three. The other part of the ascension, as I understand it, will be leaving our earth suit behind. Some of us will die before any prediction of apocalypse or end time arrives if that's what you believe. Shedding the earth suit is, however, inevitable at some point. I don't know about you, but I say thank goodness to mortality—for I'm not sure I'd want to see what my body looks like after three or four hundred years old. So unless you're planning on sticking around for a long time in your body, you might wish to do something about your vibration rate. At least look forward to feeling better, how about that?

What we do before we lose our earth suit is pretty important. This brings us back to the purpose we are here on earth. The main purpose is all about *learning* from each other. I bring this book to you to facilitate or help you in the process. Because we are all in this together as one spiritual body with Divine Father.

For instance, in one example, if we listen to and learn from those who have had NDE, we hear in a lot of the cases that when we lose our earth suit and transition to the *"other side"* that we are greeted by loved ones. Working in the health care field I have seen a number of departures from body suits take place. I have observed people preparing to transition, I have observed them speaking to someone *"on the other side"* and/or seeing someone *"from the other side"* waiting nearby their bed to take their hand.

The point is—we are all together in this incarnation on earth as one body with Divine Father.

Some of us incarnate together as groups.

This is how we run across another person and instinctually know we have met them before.

This means your spiritual evolution could just so happen to have an impact on mine. We have just gone over how our energy vibration can have an impact on each other.

Just as you would use exercise to strengthen and reshape your physical body, I'm now giving you exercises you can do to aid you in spiritual transformation.

This is a whole lot easier, by the way, if your vibration is higher.

✳ EXERCISE #1: *Practice Compassion*

It is easy to show compassion by giving from your heart. Acts of kindness to those without. By example look at what Mother Teresa did—she left the security of the Order to go out among the people of Calcutta—in her words, *"to be with the poorest of the poor."* There is no glamour or prestige to be gained by practicing compassion—but somehow it always comes back to you by touching your heart and their life.

✳ EXERCISE #2: *Practice giving love away.*

Practice giving love away to the most unexpected people. It's easy to love someone when they are acting worthy of love. It's much more difficult to apply love to unlikely souls.

This is a test of our true mettle when we can love someone in spite of their trials in life. In spite of the lessons they are also learning. Seek out to give your love to a most unlikely person, then you know you are on track. Jesus did this with the prostitute as an example for us to take to heart. Remember—in Jesus' example with the prostitute He showed her mercy and grace regardless her deeds. Our job here on earth is to recognize that every single living soul and living thing is worthy of Divine Fathers' love. If you want a better grasp on believing God and Love are synonymous try the following. For the exercise in Love repeat the following passage below to yourself. First read it with the word—Love, as it is written in the bible. Then read it a second time, inserting the word—God—where the blank line below is. Lastly, read the passage a third time, inserting your name, where the blank line is. For a friend of mine who read it to me this last way, the passage held a very powerful revelation for both of us. For owners of bibles, the passage is *1 Corinthians 13*.

_____ is patient and kind. _____ is not jealous or boastful or proud or rude. _____ does not demand its own way. _____ is not irritable, and it keeps not record of when it has been wronged. _____ is never glad about injustice but rejoices whenever the truth wins out. _____ never gives up, never loses faith, is always hopeful, and endures through every circumstance. _____ will last forever, but prophecy and speaking in tongues and special knowledge will all disappear. For even our special knowledge is incomplete, and our prophecy is incomplete. But when the end comes, these special gifts will all disappear.

It's like this: When I was a child, I spoke and thought and reasoned as a child does. But when I grew up, I put away childish things. Now we see things imperfectly as in a poor mirror, but then we will see everything with perfect clarity.

All that I know now is partial and incomplete, but then I will know everything completely [when we drop our bodies in death], just as God knows me now. There are three things that will endure—faith, hope, and love—and the greatest of these is love.

✳ EXERCISE #3: *Operate out of the place of Grace.*

This is not something you do for one hour a day and then go on about life the way you have been. Grace is the foundation out of which all things spiritual and loving manifest from. You get grace figured out and use it in your life every minute of the day or as much of the day as possible, the more you will naturally be following it with healing and love toward your fellow man and yourself. Grace is the key to unlocking your greatest potential. You will never fall short or come up empty-handed on how to handle any single relationship or challenge in life once you get a grip on how to think with grace about every single thing and circumstance. This spiritual gift can be developed and cultivated until we transgress no more against another fellow man. Even in the face of opposition, with grace you will see the other person in a compassionate perspective. A person of grace naturally attracts people to him or her. Others can't help themselves—they crave being touched by grace. Grace heals a battered and time-worn soul. Grace has so subtle a context in the bible that a person can skim right over it, but it carries a power like no other to transform your life when you are operating out of grace.

Grace gently transforms lives, it allows for human error and shows you, you are still worthy of God's love. Grace is accepting of the most retched life circumstance, the worst heinous crime—it does not condemn for any reason. Live, breathe and speak grace into life and your blessings will overflow.

Grace is the most wonderfully evoking tool a spiritual being has at their disposal to making life changing decisions all through eternity. Let it be a gauge by which you measure all responses to others. If you can't act out of grace then walk away without responding.

This spiritual gift takes some getting acquainted with, but once you start down the path of grace you will never ever want to turn back. Its energy is evocative. You'll be one with it and you'll change...you won't be able to help yourself. You'll want more grace in your life. Grace and Divine Father are one. Neither exists without the other.

This is the God I want to reacquaint you with—the one you've been perhaps deprived of by well-intentioned souls. God of unending, undying, unconditional love and acceptance. He operates within his own dynamic with Grace. Don't let Jesus' sacrifice on the cross be defiled and degraded from its original intent—to free us from bondage of feeling unworthy—past, present, and future. Our identity remains as Divine Father intended—*In His Image!*

IN HIS IMAGE. See here how pure and simple that makes things. To summarize and re-emphasize our spiritually Divine heritage, I want to retouch on the important points of this book and its purpose in your life.

FIRST THING TO REMEMBER ALWAYS…

Divine Father is spirit—thus are you and I. Thus our foundational DNA is spiritual. Yes, we take on human body DNA for a temporary earth life, but we always revert back to our natural state as spirit. And thus the cycle goes. Eternal spiritual life…punctuated by moments of human existence.

I encourage you—find yourself, regain your identity with your spiritual DNA—your rightful place with Divine Father. Learn to seek the path back to who you were created by and what's been created within you—the beauty dwelling there that has the power to bring you to tears with the unveiling—if you haven't yet realized, trust that as soon as you shed your earth body you will realize how very much you are being loved as no one other than your spiritual Father can love you.

Like no one other than your spiritual brother, Jesus, loved you.

A love born into every soul and being, no matter our earthly heritage. No one is left out. Nor should any of us ever be made to feel left out—*ever*.

If you feel the timing is right, and you feel more comfortable following traditional paths to enlightenment, then let pastor Mike Miller (fathershousefc.com) shed light on the true identity of God in your life with the true meaning in the scripture as it was intended—it will transform you for all time, for all life circumstances. See for yourself how real meaning in scripture blows the lid on judgment. Learn how amazingly God does not judge us—unfathomable as the concept to grasp—it has been under our noses all this time.

Let's say you have tried a more traditional church, but would rather find a more spiritual church. There is the Whole Life Center for Spiritual Living, which is the United Church of Religious Science (you can google this for their locations). I also ran across a website called *Holistic Networker—Your Guide to Wellness*, featured by the Spiritual Arts Institute, where you can meet the authors of *The Metaphysical Bible* at spiritualarts.org. I have personally experienced the first two church resources I've listed above and can vouch for their integrity of intent. The latter website was just one I stumbled upon in my researching efforts.

It gets down to having better interpreters who know how to literally define things for you. Old covenant way of knowledge vs. breakthrough with Jesus' sacrifice which brought with it a new covenant way of knowledge to emerge. Herein lies Divine Fathers' pristine meaning that sets us all free.

SECOND THING TO REMEMBER ALWAYS...

Yours and my mistakes and behaviors do not change the love of our Divine Father for us. Isn't it a relief to know that your mistakes, transgressions, and behaviors do not have a power to make or break you in God's eyes?

I know many of us have been beaten down by mankind's limited scope and comprehension of Father God and Jesus, so much so that we have gone along with being demeaned and degraded away from our true identity. Divine Fathers' love is without imperfections…it defies our measly grasp of true love. You think He thinks like us? Using a third of His brain? Not a chance.

We have done this to ourselves or listened to someone else tear us down and we have bought it as truth, taken it to heart, until we have devolved so far down the spiritual beingness ladder that we have forgotten where we originated from. We have tried to conform to others standards to fit in, but to our own detriment. Divine Father wants you and I, all of us free of these limitations we have imposed upon ourselves. Anyone preaching anything different may mean well, but are missing the mark entirely. Grant them grace by realizing they are just where they are at spiritually, and that you are just where you are at spiritually. After granting them more grace, simply move on to gather more truth for yourself. My point is, don't settle for being stuck with what you know as truth. Don't settle for being stuck with what you know as truth, unless you make an active decision to settle for where you are at.

If you decide to settle for where you are at, just remember Divine Father dwells within us, He has not forsaken us. He has just given us the blessing of free will—which some of us have used to forget things. You are capable, at any time you make a choice to change your decision, of reclaiming your spiritual DNA. You can reclaim your identity with a loving, non-judgmental, non-condemning Divine Father. It's your spiritual right.

Religions are sadly about separateness. They each purposely segregate themselves; make their truths the only *real* truths out there, which is antithesis to Divine Father of ALL and these segregated groups can create a perception of superiority by persons stuck in this perception. Divine Father on the other hand is not about prejudices or making oneself better than another person, better than another race. Wars are fought over religion, over trying to make someone wrong. Divine Father says, *"We are ALL created in his image."*

It is okay—if you are just starting out to discover who you are. Give yourself grace by accepting that most people will be most comfortable going with the main stream of belief—whatever religion is most popular with the family, friends, community or unit you hang out with—it is more important that you start somewhere than not at all. You are where you are at and it is neither right nor wrong—you are simply where you are at and the other person is where they are at. Don't get hung up on making others right or wrong, rather move beyond this ego-designed trap to experience the truer divine you. You now have some more tools for your Divine adventure.

THIRD THING TO REMEMBER ALWAYS...

That if you simply raise your vibration you will feel better, be better, and your thoughts will follow that energy. Crystals are an easy fix to a low vibration rate. Divine Father bestowed crystal and gems with vibrational properties to assist human vibration rates. He did this intentionally. Divine Father knew we were going to need to change our energy to change our thoughts and life. We already wear diamond wedding rings, and emerald, sapphire, and other precious stones as jewelry, so we have been introduced to crystals long before I started talking about them. What we didn't know is that they are intelligent living organisms. What we didn't expect in a thousand years, perhaps, was to be introduced to the individual vibrational frequency of stones, and how they can facilitate our needs and desires in life. A good authority on the subject of crystals is *The Crystal Bible: A Definitive Guide to Crystals*, by Judy Hall. Her book is a treasure trove of fascinating details that will enlighten even the most jaded skeptic. The Gem and Mineral shops in your area can be a wonderful adventure, as well, and you will want to visit them with your *Crystal Bible* in hand. The other site I'm fond of for my own crystal supply is VibesUp.com. This is where I went to for my crystal mat, soles for shoes, and crystal energy water container and I can personally recommend them.

Don't forget that while you are working on becoming a new and enlightened you, that you stop to have fun, go for a walk in the sunshine, play at your favorite pastime and love yourself with all your heart.

—Peace and Joy and Love to you on your exciting new journey—

Appendix A: Instruments for measuring Vibrational energy

Kirlian Photography – Photography that was accidentally discovered by Semyon Kirlian in 1939. He discovered that if an object on a photographic plate is connected to a source of high voltage, an aura or corona of electrical discharge can be photographed. This method of detecting vibration has been used to detect stress in athletes and has shown that leaves which have been picked and withered have auras that were diminishing as well. The Holistic Fair I attended not that long ago, had vendors who, for a minimal cost, could take a Kirlian photograph of your aura or charkas so you could see where your energy rated. There were all kinds of energy healers at this event.

Electrometer – I checked this out on line and maybe my search wasn't broad enough but all I could find were two websites that had what I thought I was looking for. I first checked out a website that told you how to calculate frequency in Hertz. Then I checked out a vibration generator for exciting oscillating and waves mechanically, which could reach 0 to 20k Hz frequency. I was searching for a machine that can measure megahertz.

Electroscope – These are similar to the Electrometer.

Polygraph – This is the common Lie Detector devise seen in the movies, with a graph that can register fluctuations in energy when the subject is reacting to something said. Or in the case of Cleve Backster's experiment in 1966 with the plant, the energy vibration measured was the energy vibration of a human thought, which was picked up by the plant causing the plant to react. He proved with his experiment that living organisms read and respond to a person's thoughts.

Muscle Testing – Developed by Chiropractor, George J. Goodheart in 1964, this method of testing by either the arm holding strong or weak. This is an easy and safe way of evaluating a person's imbalances and physical, spiritual, and mental needs. The test subject holds the arm out to the side of the body and horizontal to the ground.

The one doing the test applies two fingers on the wrist of the subject and asks a question that would be considered truthful—for instance, if the person has blue eyes, you can ask them if they have blue eyes. The arm holding strong, meaning it can't be pushed down with two fingers applied when testing anything asked, means the answer is truthful. Your body will respond based on the truth of the statement. Same situation if the thing being tested is beneficial to you. The arm going weak means your energy is lowered and is not beneficial to you.

Pendulum Dowsing – You can use this method to look for personal mineral deficiencies, cause of allergic reactions, energy balancing and health problem sources, best date to schedule a trip, prospection for water or lost object, etc., determining what others need from you, selecting priorities and any other question you can think of. The Pendulum is a crystal or metal object that tapers to a point and is dangled from a chain or string. You can start out by asking it to respond by saying, yes, and see which way it circles or swings back and forth. Then you do the same by asking it to respond by saying, no, and see which way it circles or swings back and forth. You can find lots of information on pendulums on the internet.

Divining Rods – Two simple metal rods with a bend at one end (long enough length beyond bend to hold each one in your hand comfortably). The practitioner using the rods will have their intention on the subject and you will be looking for energetic movement from them as you hold them above each stone or crystal.

Movement will indicate that the stone or crystal would be beneficial. No activity from the rods would be a sign that you shouldn't include that stone or crystal. The more activity you get from the rods, the more that crystal should be included.

Large Hadron Collider (Geneva, Switzerland) - According to CBS News/March 15, 2013, this was used by the European Organization for Nuclear Research (CERN) to specifically create high energy collisions to prove that the *"God Particle"* (*Higgs boson*) was what caused the "Big Bang" that created our universe many years ago—"the Higgs boson is what joins everything and gives it matter." God of course must have been smiling about our discovery, because He has utilized this particle theory phenomenon to create life.

Credence is given to Quantum mechanics for yet another way to measure energy. The Quantum mechanics the public is more familiar with is the laser and medical technologies like MRI's and PET scans to name a few. For more information go to: *cbsnew.com* and search *God Particle* or *Higgs boson*.

Appendix B: Resources for your Spiritual Journey and Bibliography

Chapter 1 – Movie, *Mother Teresa* staring Oliva Hussey, available at amazon.com

Chapter 1-5, 8, 11, 13 – Bethards, Betty, mystic and healer, author of *Be Your Own Guru,* 1982; p. 20

Chapter 2 – Braden, Gregg, best-selling author of *The God Code* and leading authority on bridging the wisdom of our past with science, medicine, and peace of our future, in collaboration with Jonathan Goldman, *Holy Harmony,* 2002, CD jacket.

Chapter 2 – Goldman, Jonathan, an internationally known writer and authority on sound healing, in collaboration with Gregg Braden's research, has developed the sound of the God code. Healing Code Tuning Forks & Ancient YHSVH Chant CD, *Holy Harmony,* 2002, CD jacket.

Chapter 2 & 10-12 – McTaggart, Lynne, who explains very neatly this "energy" whom Divine Father instilled in us in her latest book, *The Intention Experiment,* 2008: 3: p35-41. McTaggart talks about an experiment by Cleve Backster, who developed the polygraph, and who proved that plants read our thoughts.

Chapter 3 – *Holy Bible,* (NLT) John 11: 1-44. After death Lazarus did this same kind of spirit incarnating. Jesus rose him from the dead. Talking about God's Secret revealed to us in 1 Corinthians 15:51-55, is the place you can read about those who have died will be raised with transformed bodies…then we who are living will be transformed so that we will never die…when our perishable earthly bodies have been transformed into heavenly bodies that will never die.

Chapter 3 – Piper, Pastor Don, tells an inspiring NDE story and how it led to further spiritual enlightenment for him in, *90 Minutes in Heaven,* 2004.

Chapter 3 – Renowned healer, spiritual leader and Medical Doctor, Master Sha, talks about the soul enlightenment journey in his book, *Soul Wisdom,* 2008.

Chapter 3 – Definition (14c): Resurrection: Act of rising from the dead or to rise again. 1 (a) The rising of Christ from the dead. *Merriam Webster's Collegiate Dictionary,* 1999.

Chapter 3 – Definition (1858): Reincarnate: 1 (b) Rebirth in a new body or forms of life; esp. a rebirth of a soul in a new human body. 2: a fresh embodiment. *Merriam Webster's Collegiate Dictionary,* 1999.

Chapter 3 – Definition (14c): Ascension: The act or process of ascending. Ascending (1599): rising or increasing to higher levels, values or degrees. *Merriam Webster's Collegiate Dictionary*, 1999. In spiritual terms this simply means you don't die at all; there's no death process involved as we know it, except to say that you no longer have an earth body. So ascension has to do with the movement of spirit. An example would be moving from one dimension to another dimension in spirit form. We presently reside on earth in the third dimension, but there are the 4th and 5th and higher dimensions as well.

Chapter 3 – Definition (14c): <u>Incarnation:</u> (1) The embodiment of a deity or spirit in some earthly form. (14c) <u>Incarnate</u>: (1) (a) Invested with bodily and esp. human nature and form. *Merriam Webster's Collegiate Dictionary*, 1999.

Chapter 3 – Definition (15c): <u>Incursion:</u> (2) An entering in or into. (1856) <u>Incurrent</u> means to give passage to a current that flows inward. *Merriam Webster's Collegiate Dictionary*, 1999. An example would be entrance of spirit into a body.

Chapter 3 & 5 – Ritchie, George G., talks about his NDE in an Army Hospital at age 20, in his book, *Return From Tomorrow*, 1978.

Chapter 3, 5, 6 – Brinkley, Dannion, had his body zapped twice by lightning and he died once in the hospital of complications of an infection—he had total of three NDE experiences, and talks about his journey in *Saved By The Light,* 2008; and *Secrets of the Light,* 2008.

Chapter 6 & 11 – Tipping, Collin, author of, *Radical Forgiveness,* 2009; and his other book, *Radical Manifestation,* 2006; 7: p52-53. These books made sense to why the traditional forgiveness was missing the mark. If you have challenges forgiving yourself or anyone else, I find these books incredibly enlightening. Tipping talks about Ego vs Spirit from a wonderful point-of-view as a counselor.

Chapter 6-7 – Dyer, Dr. Wayne, speaks of his own personal healing experience facilitated by John of God in his book, *Wishes Fulfilled,* 2012; p110-111.

Chapter 6, 10 & 12 – Melchizedek, Drunvalo, author of volumes 1 and 2 of, *The Ancient Secret of The Flower of Life,* 1990-2000; Discusses the energy and science behind the spiritual world and he has a nice description of the energy vibration of the Mer-Ka-Ba or Lightbody. There is much discussion around his chapter on *The New Children* or another name is Indigo Children. In 1985, *Omni Magazine* was present with the Chinese Government to observe the phenomenon and found that it was true.

Chapter 7 – Ward, Dr. William A., Pastor for 65 years is another miracle facilitator who performs on a grand public scale. He is author of *Miracles That I Have Seen,* 1998, 1: p1-4

Chapter 7, 11 – Keyes, Lisa, her divine methodology of <u>Sacred Anointing Ceremony and Meditation</u>. Website: lisakeyesmdm.com

Chapter 7 – Hankins, Marsha, a channel for Universal Truth. Website: iamstandinginthelight.com.

Chapter 8, 13 – Twyman, James, sums up Spiritual vs. Religious by giving some contrasts to look at. Into the contrast and comparison arena, according to James, religious people will look for God somewhere other than in themselves. He is the author of <u>The Moses Code</u>, 2008; p94.

Chapter 9, 13 – Pastor Mike Miller of Father's House Ministries can, using literal definitions, clear up the misinterpretations using the Bible everyone else uses to shed light on Divine Father for you. They have televised services and they are a wonderful source if you don't find you're yet ready for the spiritual-minded realm and yet you find yourself weary of the path you've been walking. For more go to: fathershousefc.com.

Chapter 10 – CBS News, March 15, 2013, <u>The God Particle</u>. See more about this in Appendix A or go to <u>cbsnew.com</u>.

Chapter 10 – Lytle, Dr. Larry, author of <u>Healing Light: Energy Medicine of The Future</u>, 2008; who developed the QLazer device (soft laser therapy) based on his research on healing at a quantum, cellular level—with FDA approval for Osteoarthritis and Carpal Tunnel.

One of the many protocols he offers is a special section on Chakra Balancing with the QLaser.

Chapter 10 – Gordon, Richard, author of *Quantum Touch: The Power To Heal,* 2006; is another researcher and healer who teaches special breathing and body focusing techniques to raise your energy level.

Chapter 10 – Garripoli, Garri author of, *Qigong: Essence of The Healing Dance,* 1999; (pronounced chee gung) has studied under a renowned master of Eastern healing techniques which teaches us how to understand Qi (our bioelectric life force) to heal ourselves and others.

Chapter 10 & 11 – Howell, Kelly, creator of Brain Sync (Brain Wave Therapy), offers clinically proven brain wave therapy studied by biofeedback therapists for theta state, deep meditation. CD, *Deep Meditation,* 2003.

Chapter 11 – Tooley, Anne Christine, is the author of the, *Vibrational Energy Medicine* web site and she talks about DNA in relation to The Kabbalah Tree of Life being the blueprint of ALL life. Internet Google research.

Chapter 11 – Gerber, Richard, author of <u>Vibrational Medicine</u>, 2001; talks about how there are two fundamentally different kinds of energy, which according to William Tiller, a Stanford physicist, is evident in Tiller-Einstein model. Internet Google research.

Chapter 11 – Hawkins, David, M.D., Ph.D. is author of <u>Power vs. Force</u>, 1995-2012; and he used Applied Kinesiology and Muscle Testing to map out the Scale of Consciousness. A psychologist and consciousness researcher, he discovered that all atoms and sub-atoms were nothing more than energy and went on to write the scientifically validated doctorate dissertation that proved all objects have energy. All of this energy vibrates as listed on the model outline of how individual qualities of mind rank in terms of vibration, on a scale of 20 to 600.

Chapter 11 & 13 – Keyt, Kaitlyn, at <u>VibesUp.com</u>, has done some wonderful discoveries in the area of confirming everything is energy and has a vibration—your food, your body, even your thoughts.

She has garnered 5 Visionary Awards for her crystal products for which she has developed a special Essential Oil infused Liquid Crystal coating that she applies to all her products.

Chapter 12 – Kramarik, Akiane, featured on the Katie Couric talk show, who painted the picture she named, _Prince of Peace;_ the flawless painting of Jesus, when she was only eight years old. She is considered one of The New Children. Find her at: *artakiane.com*

Chapter 12 – Braud, Dr. William, a psychologist, and his colleagues at the Mind Science Foundation in San Antonio conducted an experiment in a lab dish, which proved that people, with their thoughts and energy, could slow down the rate that red blood cells die. Internet Google research.

Chapter 12 – Emoto, Dr. Masaru, discovered the power of crystals when he did the experiment confirming that higher vibrational words as well as low vibrational words affected water, when frozen—proof that water can read our thoughts. Internet Google research.

Chapter 13 – Hall, Judy, is a good authority on the subject of crystals. Her book is a treasure trove of fascinating details that will entertain and enlighten even the most jaded skeptic. She is the author of several books, but the one I use is, _The Crystal Bible: A Definitive Guide to Crystals_, 2003.

Appendix C: – _The History of Crystals_, at The Crystal Healing Shop at crystalhealingshop.com. Internet Google research.

Appendix C: History of Crystal Intelligence

What I've learned in college about Crystals is just the tip of the iceberg. I will try to make this entertaining as well as informational. What I tell everyone who is interested in this field of energy is to have fun researching. The place I started was with my *Crystal Bible* by Judy Hall. From there I found *VibesUp.com* and decided to take a formalized class to educate myself. The scope and reach of this subject is both humbling and fascinating at the same time. But because I chose to talk to you about Crystal Vibrational energy I thought it only helpful to give you a little history. To have included this in the body of my story would have slowed down the flow. But I'm happy to include it here for those of you whose curiosity is needing satisfied.

According to *The History of Crystals*, at The Crystal Healing Shop at: *crystalhealingshop.com*.

History records the use of crystals as functional and ornamental. The Gods of ancient myth wore them in their breastplates. Priests of many societies and brotherhoods, as keepers and preservers of lost prehistoric wisdom, often wore bejeweled amulets and plates, which acted as "oracles" and "voice pieces" from which advice was obtained. The Urim and Thummim stones of the Hebrew high priests were a prime example. The Atlanteans used crystals for healing, communication, weather control, as record keepers, among other things. Tibetans used them to produce light.

Other ancient civilizations, such as the Myans and Spanish chroniclers used "mirror" stones to direct them.

Significantly, the Incan Temple of the Sun, and the pyramid complexes of the Mayas, were all located on Earth energy lines. There is thus reason to believe that the Ancients possessed the ability of transmitting images along these lines, and crystal lenses or screens were used at specific centers to transform the images into pictures, much like a modern television set. When we examine what modern research is uncovering regarding the full spectrum of the properties of crystals, and compare this with the Ancient knowledge, we discover we are touching upon only the very beginnings of a vast forgotten technology.

Crystals have many functions of which we know of, from simplistic as storing light, converting sunlight into electricity, to storing vast amounts of information.

A cut sliver of crystal can pick up a specified vibratory pattern; the sliver can they be "frozen" and subsequently "unfrozen" later to playback the pattern.

This sounds much like the story earlier where water crystals were frozen after attaching pieces of paper with words upon the paper to the glass and the effect of vibratory pattern of the words could be seen under a microscope.

Not only, knowledge, but the actual consciousness and emotional energies of psychic individuals from past ages may still reside in many ancient crystal forms. Several researchers have used crystals to capture the life force, or the vibratory pattern of a person at death. Other experiments being conducted are said to have successfully captured a human thought within a crystal and retransmitted it back as an image.

Author George Hunt Williamson, believes that crystals can think and that many of the megaliths or standing stones have an "intelligence" within them. There is evidence that certain individual crystals like diamonds and other precious stones can hold conscious emotional energies from bygone eras, which may be triggered from time to time, affecting their owners. One example given is the famous Hope Diamond (a piece of the original Great Blue Diamond), which had a reputation for imparting a mysterious curse so that every owner, even those who have handled it, have been subject to misfortune, tragedy or violent death. This diamond was, in the name of revenge, infused with a negative consciousness or emotional pattern by the priests of the temple, along with Mogul Emperor Auranzeb.

For this reason, we need to respect the proper crystal clearing techniques; which vary depending upon your personal preference and the type of crystal. I simply lay the crystals I use for energy vibration work upon a Selenite crystal. Selenite and Carnelian are two of the self-cleansing crystals and can clear other stones and crystals as well.

It has occurred to me that you might like to know that when you go shopping for jewelry like diamonds, emeralds, sapphire, and other precious stones it wouldn't be a bad idea to clear the energy that might be attached to these stones with all the handling by customers and thoughts that may be floating around a jewelry store. Always cleanse jewelry that comes to you from someone else, as it can hold their negative vibrations and pass them on to you. The clearing techniques most widely used are smudging with smoke (sage incense works well), passing the crystal through the light from a candle, laying jewels upon the self-cleansing crystals I mentioned above, or if you are good at visualizing, then you can visualize them surrounded by light, which purifies and re-energizes them. There are other methods like running them under water or immersed in sea water or salt water and rinsed, but as you do this hold the intention that all negativity will be washed away and the crystal reenergized.

Then there are the VibesUp.com crystals which are infused with a Liquid Crystal-Essential oil Plant Botanical which has its own coating of tiny Quartz Spheres that work to attract specific good energies and regenerate themselves. The internet is a wonderful tool to finding anything you want to know about crystals.

Appendix D: Scale of Consciousness (Pocket Guide)

This information is from the book, *Power vs. Force*, by David Hawkins, M.D., Ph.D. This model outlines how individual qualities of mind rank in terms of vibration, on a scale of 20 to 600. Dr. Hawkins has researched how the vibration rates affect us. There is more on this scale of consciousness and its effects on us in Chapter 11.

QUALITY	LOG	EMOTION
Peace	600	Bliss
Joy	540	Serenity
Love	500	Reverence
Reason	400	Understanding
Acceptance	350	Forgiveness
Willingness	310	Optimism
Neutrality	250	Trust
Courage	200	Affirmation
Pride	175	Scorn
Anger	150	Hate
Desire	125	Craving
Fear	100	Anxiety
Grief	75	Regret
Apathy	50	Despair
Guilt	30	Blame
Shame	20	Humiliation

About the Author

LIGHTWORKER AND VIBRA~LIGHT HEALING PRACTITIONER, GRACE LIGHTCHILD, is a former award-winning, best-selling author of Women's Fiction. After a break from her fiction writing career to finish her college degree, Grace woke up one day and realized she was finished reading text books and eagerly delved into her greatest passion yet—Spirit vibration. Her caring heart and love of humanity has transitioned from writing about the power of love in fiction to writing about true-life Divine love, grace, and compassion. Her story is a six-year journey of self-actualization where the accumulation of years spent pouring through divine spiritual documentation by people of all walks of life, to discovering new breakthroughs in the blend of science and spirituality brought her one discovery after another. This book is a heartfelt project guided by divine spirit to awaken and inspire humanity.

Grace tells how she has always felt something about life the way it was being taught was a little off kilter, and now that Divine Spirit has aligned her vibration, she's excited to bring you her very own true story of vibration transformation.

Grace has been featured on WB2 Today Show and spoken to sold-out audiences coast to coast.

- ✻ WWW.GRACELIGHTCHILD.COM
- ✻ WWW.LINKEDIN.COM/GRACELIGHTCHILD
- ✻ WWW.FACEBOOK.COM/GRACELIGHTCHILD